'*Touched by God's Spirit* explores the compelling nature and gift of welcoming wise spiritual guides, living and dead, into the complexity of our mortal and spiritual lives. Luke's wise analysis of the gifts of Henri's mentors, combined with Henri's journey of integration, become a "Way" towards becoming more truly human.'

Sue Mosteller, Founder of the Henri Nouwen Legacy Trust

'An intense and scholarly evaluation of a great spiritual master which makes an invaluable contribution to the field of contemporary spirituality.'

Dr Michael Ford, biographer of Henri Nouwen

'This study of the life and work of Henri Nouwen, a prolific author, known for his pastoral and spiritual insight, is important for two main reasons. It shows how the "wounded healer" made his own tough pilgrimage from narrowly defined securities to an inner and outer displacement which opened his heart to "others" of all kinds, while also demonstrating how deeply significant for that journey was the influence of those described as his "mentors". Communion across time and space with these key figures, Merton and Vanier, Van Gogh and Rembrandt – people Nouwen knew almost entirely through their writing and their art rather than immediate presence – is what generated compassion in the inner depths of Nouwen's inner solitariness, and opened him to living it out in community with the poorest of the poor, people with profound learning disabilities.'

Frances Young, British theologian, Methodist minister, and Emeritus Professor at the University of Birmingham

'In this breakthrough work, Fr. Luke has spotlighted so brightly the unexplored heart of compassion Nouwen possessed---as impacted by four diverse figures: Merton, van Gogh, Vanier, and Rembrandt. Indeed we become like the very people we allow to influence us the most.'

Wil Hernandez, PhD, Obl.OSB, author of *Mere Spirituality: The Spiritual Life According to Henri Nouwen*

'Henri Nouwen's compassionate voice speaks prophetically to an anxious, success-driven Western culture. In this insightful and lucid text Luke Penkett draws deeply on the 'Nouwen canon' to articulate a humane, compassionate Christian spirituality for this generation.'

Right Reverend Jonathan Frost, Bishop of Southampton

Touched by God's Spirit

How Merton, van Gogh, Vanier and
Rembrandt influenced Henri Nouwen's
heart of compassion

Luke Penkett

With a Foreword by Rowan Williams

DARTON · LONGMAN + TODD

First published in 2019 by
Darton, Longman and Todd Ltd
1 Spencer Court
140 – 142 Wandsworth High Street
London SW18 4JJ

ISBN: 978-0-232-53385-9

A catalogue record for this book is available from the British Library

Phototypeset by Kerrypress Ltd, St Albans, Hertfordshire, AL3 8JL
Printed and bound in Great Britain by Short Run Press Ltd, Exeter

For Paul Sampson,
carer, companion

Contents

Foreword

Some 'spiritual' writers speak out of an assured and calm authority; reading them, we are able to immerse ourselves in a vision that has been matured and rounded out, a vision that moves and holds us because of its fullness. Henri Nouwen was not quite like that: his writing shows its workings, shows him growing and maturing, shows his uncertainties and insecurities. His life is one of frustrations and fresh starts, characterised by frank admissions of his own neediness. It would be quite wrong to say that he reinvented himself: he was in all kinds of ways remarkably consistent and faithful to a vision. But he has a restlessness about him, as a person and as a writer, which means that we can't look to his biography for a pattern of steady achievement or advance. To the end he remains awkward, hungry for intimacy, with an almost childlike transparency to his own unfinished labour with himself.

And this is what makes him such a powerful and beloved guide to the life of the spirit. As he himself was to underline again and again, we may begin by thinking we are sent to bring good news to the poor; but until we recognise that we are the poor to whom the good news is to come, we are stuck in dramas of spiritual heroism that will do no good to us or those we want to serve. Compassion begins here, in this acknowledgment of our own poverty and confusion, our unwelcome solidarity with a 'poor' world where human beings are lost and wounded. Nouwen's hunger for love and stability, for greater spiritual anchorage or depth, expressed with raw clarity in so many books, tells the reader straight away that this is someone who – like the incarnate Lord himself – begins his ministry simply by letting us know he shares our world. In his last years as a member of a L'Arche community, he recognised more and more clearly that just sharing a world with the vulnerable was in some strange way the supreme task laid before him – not preaching, not writing, not guiding and serving in obvious ways, but learning to be a patient companion to the Christ he met in those he lived with.

This study of Nouwen as a theologian of compassion brings him to life as an incarnational witness to the gospel which speaks of God's patient companionship in a world of all kinds of poverty. When we are tempted to encourage ourselves with stories of triumphant eloquent proclamation, dramatic selflessness and spiritual or intellectual brilliance, this is a story whose shape draws us back to the basic form of Christian storytelling itself, the story of divine identification with us.

ROWAN WILLIAMS
July 2018

Acknowledgements

Ten years ago I began to share my life with people who live and work in L'Arche, an international federation of houses and communities for people with and without learning disabilities. As assistant, priest and monk, living and working alongside people from various denominational and faith backgrounds and none, I was immediately presented with issues around ecumenism and multi-faith collaboration and worship. Much of my first year in L'Arche was spent in discovering the spiritual, pastoral and liturgical needs of its core members and assistants and it was a natural step when desiring to do some academic work to look at ecumenism within and without L'Arche.

At the same time, I was occupied in founding the Henri Nouwen Society in the United Kingdom with a fine committee of dedicated men and women – some of whom had known Henri personally – and the enthusiastic support of the Henri Nouwen Society in North America and Canada. My academic interests were being formed and soon I started to explore the possibility of researching ecumenism in the life and writing of Henri J. M. Nouwen out of which seeds of the present book took root and grew.

I was richly blessed in having Frances M. Young as my supervisor. Frances knows the work of L'Arche both nationally and internationally, and it is a very great joy to acknowledge with gratitude her abiding encouragement and generous guidance throughout the preparation of my thesis.

I am grateful, also, to have the opportunity of recording my thanks to Mike Ford, a fine Nouwen scholar and dear friend, whose enthusiasm for his subject must be blamed at least in part for kindling my own passion for the same subject matter!

During the preparation of my thesis I enjoyed the immense privilege and pleasure of discussing particular points with a number of stimulating scholars and I especially wish to thank Fr John Eudes Bamberger OCSO, Mary Bastedo, Christopher de Bono, Cliff Edwards, Jim Forest, Wil Hernandez, Michael W. Higgins, Gregory Jensen, Deirdre LaNoue, Donald P. McNeill, Sr Sue Mosteller CSJ, Peter Naus, Jean Vanier and Maureen Wright.

I should like to express my appreciation, too, to Gabrielle Earnshaw of The Henri J.M. Nouwen Archives and Research Collection, John M. Kelly Library, University of St Michael's College in the University of Toronto who not only made her holdings available for consultation, but was most generous in her time, interest, and help.

Nobody could have been blessed with more compassionate examiners than I for my viva voce. David Ford and Philip Sheldrake assured me within the first few minutes of my viva that I had passed and that there was not to be any rewriting and then spent the remainder of our time together happily discussing how the thesis could be prepared for publication. Their belief in it and in me was the most tremendous encouragement.

It was while Rowan Williams was Archbishop of Canterbury that, together with the Council for the Archbishop's Examination in Theology, he introduced an MPhil research degree, with the opportunity of extending the candidate's research to a PhD. I'm profoundly grateful to Dr Williams, not only for his generous support extending back over a number of years, but also for his illuminating Foreword to the present publication.

During the last couple of years I have enjoyed the friendship and expertise of David Moloney and Virginia Hearn, of Darton, Longman, and Todd, who have courteously and skilfully formed the book out of my thesis for publication.

Retiring from L'Arche in October, 2012, because of increasing blindness, and handing over the work of the Henri Nouwen Society in the United Kingdom to another for the same reason, I moved to Dorset and throughout the past seven years I have been indebted to Paul Sampson, my carer and companion, who has unstintingly provided the peace of mind and environment necessary for the completion of, firstly, my doctoral thesis and, now, this book.

LUKE PENKETT
September 2018

Introduction

Henri Nouwen was an internationally acclaimed priest, spiritual director and writer. He was admired as a professor at some of the most prestigious American universities and beloved by many who not only knew him personally but also by those who continue to read his books today. Nouwen published 39 books during his lifetime – a further three were published posthumously – and corresponded regularly with hundreds of friends in English, Dutch, French, German and Spanish and reached thousands through his words. Now a new generation still turns to his writings in order to be refreshed, to grow, and to discover.

One of Nouwen's finest books, *Compassion*, co-authored in 1982 with Donald P. McNeill and Douglas A. Morrison, was published again in 2008 and is still highly regarded as a masterly exposition of the role of compassion in our everyday lives. As we are bombarded daily by scenes of horrific violence on our televisions, hear of tragedies on our radios, and read disturbing stories in our newspapers, we are left wondering not only how we can respond but also how we can protect ourselves from emotional or psychological burn-out.

For Nouwen, and for millions like him, compassion was and remains a significant part of his – and our own – lives. *Touched by God's Spirit* is a footnote to *Compassion*, seeking out – and finding – the nature and nurture of compassion in the soul of Henri Nouwen, exploring below the skin, if you like, the main influences on Nouwen and discovering those aspects of compassion that were of most importance to him.

Four key mentors had a profound influence on Henri, and the present book investigates the synthesis which Nouwen made of their influences, particularly with regard to his understanding of compassion. In so doing, a *lacuna* can be filled in both the study of Nouwen and in the appreciation of the role compassion can play in all our lives. These mentors were Thomas Merton, Vincent van Gogh, Jean Vanier, and Rembrandt van Rijn. Each of these mentors, in their own way, anticipated Nouwen's work of retrieving an authentically Christian vision of the world, and certain theological common concepts – discovering solidarity with people, being downwardly mobile, acting compassionately, and resting in God – emerge as they did so.

Two of these mentors, Merton and Vanier, Nouwen knew personally. The other two – Van Gogh and Rembrandt – were only known to Nouwen through their painting and, in Van Gogh's case, his writing as well. Others could equally have been chosen for this book (in addition to those psychologists and psychotherapists that were the focus of Nouwen's early career):[1] the Desert Fathers and Mothers, Mother Teresa of Calcutta, and Gustavo Gutiérrez, the Peruvian father of liberation theology whose books Nouwen read avidly, to name but a few. However, I have chosen these four mentors, because their influence on Nouwen was *longer and deeper* than most, as evidenced by his returning to them repeatedly in his teaching and writing throughout his later career.

Nouwen encountered Merton in May, 1967. He began to learn about the art and writing of Van Gogh in 1975. He met Vanier in 1981. The painting of the *Prodigal Son* Nouwen came across in 1983.

Compassion is the unifying element, running like a thread that gradually becomes visible, in the life and work of each of these four very different mentors. Yet, perhaps, it is not until all four are considered together that the extent and significance of the role that compassion plays in their lives is fully understood. Secondary literature has already looked at these mentors individually,[2] but here – for the first time – they are considered together, their work thus emerging as a kind of unifying presence and theological wellspring in Nouwen's own life and writing, catalysing, centring, and nurturing his outreach to others in compassionate dialogue, friendship and community.

A hitherto unpublished integrated chronological bibliography of Nouwen's primary writing[3] is presented at the end of the final chapter. It will serve as a useful reference tool for the book proper, providing biographical[4] and literary reference points beyond the immediate foci of the chapters.

Compassion: A Reflection on the Christian Life was written over the course of five years. It's a book that examines human compassion as the manifestation of the love of God. Based on Paul's Christological hymn in the second chapter of his letter to the Christians at Philippi, *Compassion* was considered by Jurjen Beumer (1947–2013), Nouwen's first biographer, to be 'his most theological book. Reflections on spiritual concepts are more firmly grounded here than anywhere else.'[5] It is a challenging work, meriting a sustained study as a classic of contemporary Christian ethics, not only for its account of lessons learnt about God's love, but also for its teaching on living the compassionate life. 'Compassion asks us to go where it hurts, to enter into places of pain, to share in brokenness, fear, confusion, and anguish. Compassion challenges us to cry out with those in misery, to mourn with those who are lonely, to weep with those in tears. Compassion requires us to be weak with the weak, vulnerable with the vulnerable, and powerless with the powerless.'[6] The book reflects Nouwen's growing interest in social issues and the challenge for Christians to be lights in the darkness.

Compassion was the last book that Nouwen worked on during his time at Yale. McNeill, Morrison and Nouwen – all Roman Catholics – had met at a small Greek restaurant in Washington D.C., in the early to mid 1970s, and all shared a common discontent with the individualism and spiritual dryness at their universities: McNeill at Notre Dame, Morrison at Catholic University, and Nouwen at Yale.

> As we sat in the empty subterranean dining room expressing our discontent with the individualism and spiritual dryness of our academic lives … the three of us found ourselves scribbling notes on our table napkins. This time, unlike many others, our complaints led not to idleness but to a plan.[7]

That plan was to meet on nine Thursdays to study and pray together. The most urgent question that presented itself as a matter for study to the three theologians was how to live compassionately:

> Being teachers of pastoral theology and finding ourselves in the city where great political power is sought, acquired, and exercised, the question of how to live compassionately in our world presented itself as the most urgent question for our meetings.[8]

'These reflections on compassion' the authors write in their Preface, 'have emerged from those nine Thursday meetings.'[9] The book was stimulated by Christ's injunction to be compassionate: 'Be compassionate as your Father is compassionate' (Lk 6:36). This injunction is the perspective of the book and the authors explicitly state that the book is offered 'in the deep conviction that through compassion our humanity grows into its fullness.'[10] It is a challenge. A radical challenge to all Christians. 'A call that goes right against the grain; that turns us completely around and requires a total conversion of heart and mind. It is indeed a radical call, a call that goes to the roots of our lives.'[11]

Nouwen is internationally acclaimed as one of the most beloved and important spiritual writers of the second half of the twentieth century. His books, translated into countless foreign languages and published in innumerable editions, are considered as spiritual classics, as relevant today as they were when they were first published, if not more so. Yet, little has been written on Nouwen's own mentors, especially on those who influenced him the most and whose influence lasted for a significant period of Nouwen's life.

In bringing these four masters of the spiritual life together, their considerable contribution, notably, to compassionate Christian living is studied in depth.

Nouwen's priestly ministry was underscored by integrating his deep knowledge of Christian spirituality with his ground-breaking studies in psychology. His insights into the human person – self-revealing without being exhibitionist about his own struggles, deeply sensitive to human weakness, and having the ability to connect – enabled him to keep his ministry on a vitally inter-personal level and, thereby, he gained a greater awareness of the potentialities that may arise as a consequence of a compassionate outlook.

In his book *Church Dogmatics* Karl Barth (1886-1968), arguably one of the greatest Protestant theologians of the twentieth century, describes the downward pull that characterises Jesus' compassion, and this description is cited in the book *Compassion* in order to illustrate Jesus' *kenosis*.[12] Barth writes that Jesus moves from 'the heights to the depth, from victory to defeat, from riches to poverty, from triumph to suffering, from life to death.'[13] In Christ compassion is no bending, no reaching toward the underprivileged from the status of privilege, no superficial gesture but an absolute and unconditional love, totally without reserve. 'Not a movement away from God, but a movement toward God: A God for us who came not to rule but to serve.'[14] If this is the example of compassion God sets before Christians, then Christians, too, ought to participate in this humbling self-emptying, and it is in this self-emptying that compassion is engendered.

> By setting out with Jesus on the road of the cross, we become people in whose lives the compassionate presence of God in this world can manifest itself.[15]

Compassion, then, is nothing less than a way of life, a crucial response to the vocation to live as a Christian, with important lessons that have significant implications for the future of each one of us.

Chapter 1

Thomas Merton, monk, contemplative, poet

What is it that causes any one of us to go searching for an advisor, a consultant, a guru, a mentor? It might be in order to seek help for a specific short-term problem; to request a second opinion; to gain enlightenment; to discover a way forward. It was most probably the last of these reasons that caused Henri Nouwen to set off for the Abbey of Our Lady of Gethsemani in pursuit of one of the monks who had been there since December 1941, Thomas Merton. By May 1967, the year in which Nouwen met his mentor, Merton had published *The Seven Storey Mountain* and received, in addition to critical acclaim, a voluminous and never-ending amount of fan mail. He had begun teaching the novices at Gethsemani, a responsibility that he deeply enjoyed. And he was now living in a hermitage within the grounds of the abbey. By 1967, too, Nouwen had just completed two years as a Fellow in the programme for Religion and Psychiatry at the Menninger Clinic in Kansas and had become Visiting Professor in the Psychology Department in the University of Notre Dame, Indiana. At a time when America was dominated by race riots and the war in Vietnam, Nouwen was determined to discover how Merton freed himself from the pre-occupations of discrimination, poverty and violence and, as an American citizen, could live as a contemplative monk and poet.

At the same time as pursuing his studies in psychology, Nouwen was attracted to the monastic life, partly because of his need for a regulated life, partly because of his need for the discipline that a community might offer him, both of which were lacking from his life and work. It therefore comes as no surprise that Nouwen was drawn to Gethsemani and, in particular, to Merton.

There were a number of writers that Henri Nouwen drew on who influenced his spiritual development and whom he acknowledges in his own prolific output. Arguably the writer from whom he learned most was

Thomas Merton (1915-68). As Michael O'Laughlin comments in his book *God's Beloved, A Spiritual Biography of Henri Nouwen*, the only biographical account of Nouwen's life and works to be authorized by Nouwen's Legacy Trust, both men were 'revolutionary writers who advanced creatively through their chosen subjects. Both stood within the bounds of Catholicism looking out at the world around them.'[1]

During the years 1966 to 1968, while he was Visiting Professor in the Psychology Department at the University of Notre Dame, South Bend, Indiana,[2] Nouwen journeyed to the Abbey of Our Lady of Gethsemani, Kentucky, in order to meet Merton. The meeting took place on 7 May 1967, and was to be of seminal importance for Henri. Later, having taught at Notre Dame, during which time two books – *Intimacy: Pastoral Psychological Essays*,[3] and *Creative Ministry: Beyond Professionalism in Teaching, Preaching, Counselling, Organizing and Celebrating*[4] – were completed, Nouwen returned to the Netherlands,[5] and there wrote a further two books, both in his mother tongue, *Bidden om het Leven, Het Contemplatief engagement van Thomas Merton*,[6] and *Mit Open Handen: Notities over het gebed*.[7] The first of this pair was translated into English by David Schlaver with the assistance of Nouwen and published, first under the title *Pray to Live*, next as *Thomas Merton: Contemplative Critic*, and then, finally, as *Encounters with Merton: Spiritual Reflections*. In this ground-breaking work Nouwen dealt with the life and thought of Thomas Merton. Although Merton and Nouwen met only once, the spirituality of the older man (Merton was seventeen years Nouwen's senior) was to influence Nouwen profoundly.

'[*Pray to Live* was] meant,' Nouwen wrote in his Introduction to the book, 'to be an introduction to … Thomas Merton,'[8] and was one of the first books to be published on the subject, before Merton became a household name, uncovering 'a few main trends in Merton's richly diverse and very productive life, in order to help in a better understanding of his commitment to a contemplative critique of himself and his world.'[9] It was a work that was to enjoy continued interest over the following four decades. After Nouwen had taught a class at Yale Divinity School on Merton, the book was re-edited and published under the title *Thomas Merton: Contemplative Critic* in 1981. Ten years later the book was further re-edited and published under the same title. In these early editions the book was divided into two halves – the first comprised *ter kennismaking* (*For Instruction* – consisting of Nouwen's introductory commentary), the second *ter overweging* (*For Meditation* – containing extended excerpts from Merton's works). In 2004 the book was revised by Sue Mosteller and Maureen Wright of the Henri Nouwen Center and reissued posthumously under the title *Encounters with Merton: Spiritual Reflections*. In this latest edition the two halves were integrated and, since

Merton's work had become so much more widely available than was the case in the 1970s, the lengthier excerpts, or those with cultural references requiring more detailed explanation in the earlier editions, were removed or abridged. Nouwen's reflections received minor editing for style, gender inclusive language, and sociological terms but nothing of his original content was omitted.

The book was an impressive piece of writing and Nouwen was considered by those who knew Merton well to have made 'broad and judicious use of the material available to him,'[10] to have touched the heart of Merton's life and work. John Eudes Bamberger (1926-),[11] Trappist monk, psychiatrist, and, in time, the fourth abbot of Genesee Abbey, the daughter house of Gethsemani, was to comment in his own Preface to the second edition of 1981:

> Henri Nouwen met Merton but once, yet by a sympathy of feeling and perception he has understood the central motivation force of Merton's life: meditation and prayer. He has seen this more truly and profoundly than some who, while claiming to be intimate friends of Merton, have altogether missed the point of his work and life through lack of feeling for his vision of God, humanity, and the cosmos. There is nothing surprising in this fact. True understanding depends not only on intelligence and proximity but above all on the heart.[12]

In preparation for his journey Nouwen submerged himself in Merton's diaries, 'the consummate record of his daily struggles, joys, aspirations, and personal defects.'[13] Indeed, Nouwen observes in *Pray to Live* that Merton was his own reporter, placing his daily feelings and thoughts under the microscope and discovering there, in the depth of his solitude, not only God but also other human beings. 'This cleansing was necessary before he could detach himself from his preoccupations to touch the world – which was being wrenched apart by racial discrimination, violence, and poverty – with the hand of compassion.'[14]

'A true guide to the heart of God and the heart of this world'

Henri Nouwen describes his encounter with Thomas Merton with increasing detail, in five places. The first of these descriptions appears in a letter of unknown date to Annet van Lindenberg, a Dutch student researching Nouwen's work. Here, Nouwen writes:

> I met [Merton] once, on the grounds of the Abbey of Gethsemani in Kentucky. Since then his person and work have had so much influence on me that his sudden death hit me like the death of one of my best friends.[15]

On that Sunday, 7 May 1967, Nouwen visited the Trappist Abbey of Our Lady of Gethsemani near Bardstown, Kentucky, in Nelson County, some 350 miles from South Bend, in order to meet 'his spiritual hero.'[16] Merton, then at the height of his fame, was barely nineteen months away from his death. It was at a time when Nouwen had completed his theological training, had met with Anton Boisen (1876–1965), an American chaplain and a leading figure in the hospital chaplaincy and clinical pastoral education movements, and was nearing the end of the first of two academic years as Visiting Professor in the Psychology Department at the University of Notre Dame, Indiana.

Merton also records the meeting. There is a reference in *Learning to Love*, Volume 6 of *The Journals of Thomas Merton*.[17] In his diaries, upon which the *Journals* are based, Merton recalls Nouwen's name incorrectly, alluding to him as Father Nau. This was amended in the published work:

> Yesterday the new Archbishop McDonough was here – I did not go to hear him speak. Ran into Raymond's friend Alexis[18] – the South African from Notre Dame – and Fr. [Henri] Nouwen (Dutch psychologist teaching at N[otre] D[ame]), had a good talk in the evening by the lake in Charlie O'Brien's pasture (old name for St Bernard's field).

The reference in Merton's diaries may be considered a cursory one at best.

On the other hand, Nouwen's recollection of the event, as recorded in the Introduction to his *Pray to Live* (published in 1972, by which time Nouwen was at Yale), the second of the four descriptions, is 'more personally felt and significant' and tells us a little more about Merton's influence on Nouwen:[19]

> I met him only once, at the Abbey of Our Lady of Gethsemani in Kentucky. Yet thereafter, his person and work had such an impact on me, that his sudden death stirred me as if it were the death of one of my closest friends. It therefore seems natural for me to write for others about the man who has inspired me most in recent years.[20]

This second description is, obviously, very similar to Nouwen's letter to van Lindenberg, both referring to Merton's influence, or 'impact', and here acknowledging the fact that Merton was the man 'who [had] inspired [Nouwen] most' during the 1960s.

A few years later, Nouwen was to describe the meeting for the third time, and in much greater detail. Opening his Foreword to James Finley's *Merton's Palace of Nowhere* (published in 1978, when Nouwen was Scholar-in-Residence at the Pontifical North American College in Rome), Nouwen hints, probably subconsciously, at their similarity:

The only time I met Thomas Merton, I was struck by his utter earthiness. While on a retreat at the Abbey of Gethsemani, two students from the University of Notre Dame who had made an appointment to meet Merton at the lakeside asked me to join them. It was a very chatty encounter. We talked a little about abbots, a little about Camus and a little about writing. We drank beer, stared into the water, and let some time pass in silence – nothing very special, profound, or 'spiritual'. In fact, it was a little disappointing. Maybe I had expected something unusual, something to talk about with others or to write home about. But Thomas Merton proved to be a very down-to-earth, healthy human being who was not going to perform to satisfy our curiosity. He was one of us.[21]

By then, it appears, Nouwen had recovered somewhat from Merton's untimely death and was seemingly less in awe of his hero. It is significant, I think, that Nouwen doesn't refer to their meeting in his Foreword to the Quaker educationalist Parker J. Palmer's *In the Belly of a Paradox: A Celebration of Contradictions in the Thought of Thomas Merton*, published in 1979.

The fourth description of the meeting comes in 1992, when Nouwen refers to his reluctance in meeting Thomas Merton, in his Foreword to Esther de Waal's *A Seven Day Journey with Thomas Merton*:

Merton himself was a very earthy as well as a very spiritual man. My own encounter with Merton is a good illustration of this. In 1966 while spending a few days at the Abbey of Gethsemani, Joe Ahearn, a friend from the University of Notre Dame, who also was a guest, said: 'I am going to see Thomas Merton this afternoon, would you like to join me?' Strangely enough I was not very eager to meet Merton. I had read The Seven Storey Mountain years ago in Holland, but no other of Merton's books and I wasn't sure if I had anything to say to him or ask him. But Joe insisted: 'Come' he said, 'you will enjoy meeting Tom. He told me to get a six-pack of beer and meet him at the pond.'

A few hours later the three of us got together. Merton looked like a farmer interrupting his work in the barn. He was dressed in blue jeans and a workman's shirt and talked in a very down-to-earth way about people and events that came up in the conversation. Nothing pious, nothing 'spiritual', nothing very 'uplifting'. It really seemed that Merton did everything to make us forget that he was one of the most known and respected spiritual writers of his time. There was a bit of a 'naughty boy' about him, someone who was not too happy with the adults and looked for little ways to get around them.

I forgot most of what we talked about. Only vague memories of a discussion on Albert Camus and some speculations about the next Abbot of Gethsemani remain in my mind. What I will always retain however is the image of this big, open, utterly normal man, who enjoyed a can of beer with two of his guests.

Less than two years later Merton was dead. Only then my seemingly insignificant hour with him started to bear fruit. Our chance meeting made me read all his books, and I discovered that this ordinary man was a true guide to the heart of God and the heart of this world.[22]

The fifth and briefest description comes in the closing months of Nouwen's life, as he writes in his Introduction to Merton's *Life and Holiness*, 'Reading this book brought back to mind my one and only encounter with Merton in a brief meeting during a visit I made to the Abbey of Gethsemani. There was a no-nonsense quality about him. Direct, open, unsentimental, and always with a twinkle in his eye. That's how Merton was. That's how this book is.'[23]

'Restoration of right order and peace ... through deep prayer'

A bright chapter in Nouwen's life began in 1971 when Colin W. Williams, the new Dean of Yale University's Divinity School, in New Haven, Connecticut, the home of the third oldest university in the United States, and a Protestant institute, invited him to visit the School.[24] Williams had read *Intimacy* and was determined to engage Nouwen as a member of faculty, an unexpected and far-sighted move.[25] After first declining the invitation because of loyal ties with the Catholic Church in the Netherlands,[26] Nouwen revisited the Yale campus and, struck by the calibre of the students – from a variety of denominations – started to teach there in the autumn of 1971, as a member of a two-person team working in pastoral ministry, the other member being James E. Dittes, Professor of Pastoral Theology and Psychology. Nouwen was to teach psychology. In the end, the initial project never came to fruition. Nouwen's passion for psychology was, however, waning, and being replaced by a desire to weave personal spirituality back into pastoral ministry. Indeed, at this point, spirituality became Nouwen's primary focus and Dittes became responsible for psychology. Nouwen's appointment, along with that of Sr Margaret Farley (later Professor of Ethics and now Professor Emerita at Yale Divinity School) broke new ground in that they were the first two full-time Roman Catholic appointments to the Protestant faculty. They were to become, in many people's hearts, the two most popular members of staff.

Sr Margaret recalls:

Henri was not exactly what Yale Divinity School had expected. This was a time when spirituality was still suspect among Protestants but now, across the United States and the world, it has become a primary concern of all religious denominations – and Henri was a major figure in all of that. His presence here, from the moment he began, was so charismatic that he immediately awakened students in a way that was phenomenal. That sometimes made it difficult for him to relate to his faculty colleagues, and not all of them appreciated him.[27]

During his time at Yale (1971-81) Nouwen taught classes on pastoral care and counselling, discipline and discipleship, ministry to the elderly and prisoners, ministry in non-religious institutions (a field based course), ministry as hospitality, the ministry of Vincent van Gogh, the relationship between ministry and spirituality, the history of spirituality, monasticism, compassion, hesychasm, desert spirituality and contemporary ministry, spiritual life and spiritual direction – and the life and work of Thomas Merton.

Living in Carriage House, one of Yale's homes, during his second year there, Nouwen entertained a wealth of interdenominational and inter-faith friends: Russian Orthodox priests, Jewish Rabbis, and right-wing evangelical Protestants. A parallel with *Conjectures of a Guilty Bystander* comes to mind here. Merton reflects:

> If I can unite in myself the thought and the devotion of Eastern and Western Christendom, the Greek and the Latin Fathers, the Russians with the Spanish mystics, I can prepare in myself the reunion of divided Christians. From that secret and unspoken unity in myself can eventually come a visible and manifest unity of all Christians ... We must contain all divided worlds and transcend them in Christ.[28]

What do Nouwen's writings on Merton reveal about the latter's response to the world in which he found himself? How does Nouwen respond to this? These questions have been succinctly answered by Bamberger in his Preface to *Pray to Live*:

> Restoration of right order and peace in the world was for Merton the fruit of the vision of God arrived at through deep prayer. Henri Nouwen has seen Merton in this perspective, and this book clearly reveals some of the concrete, practical consequences of this way of experiencing life.[29]

The five chapters of *Pray to Live* concern contemplation, silence, solitude, social justice and the wisdom of the East. Nouwen introduces his readers to *The Sign of Jonas* and *Conjectures of a Guilty Bystander*, two of Merton's diaries that cover the years 1942-52 and 1956-65 respectively, years during which Merton lived as a member of the community at Gethsemani, remaining 'a journalist, a reporter who observed the world in which he lived, but under the critical eye of the Gospel.'[30] And the amount Merton wrote is prolific — more than thirty-five books, and a staggering number of articles, in addition to many journals, and letters that have come to light, again posthumously.

During the 1940s Merton had experienced a developing awareness of a new depth of solitude and a change in the understanding of his vocation as author. His writing had enabled him to enter into a greater silence and solitude. By May 1951, after eighteen months of sickness and depression, Merton became the spiritual director for the students at Gethsemani. He discovered a profound shift in himself which was to take him from his heady university intellectual and hipster days to monk, contemplative, and poet.

Nouwen makes the astute comment that 'The silence and solitude had buried themselves so deeply in his heart that he was in the position to take on a very deep and intimate relation with other persons.'[31] According to Nouwen, who wrote the Foreword to Palmer's *In the Belly of a Paradox*, appearing a year after the publication of *Merton's Palace of Nowhere*, the genius of Merton was his balance of 'silence and solitude' with passion for life: 'If we are always thinking about contemplation, contemplation, contemplation,' Merton once wrote, 'We overlook the ordinary, authentic, real experiences of everyday life as things to enjoy ... ' Merton had the humility to perceive and accept that God is truly 'the One who cannot be caught, grasped, or understood but only intuited and recognized with a smile.'[32] Nouwen was intensely influenced by this dynamic balance between silence and solitude and the passion for life. This was a balance that Nouwen was to write about not only in his *Pray to Live* but also, more personally, in *Reaching Out* and in *The Genesee Diary: Report from a Trappist Monastery*. *The Genesee Diary*, dedicated to 'all contemplative men and women who by their commitment to unceasing prayer offer us hope in the midst of a troubled world,' was the consequence of Nouwen's six-month sojourn at that monastery in 1974 in order to test his vocation as monk. The *Diary* has been described as 'a modest simulation of Merton's great journal, *The Sign of Jonas*.'[33] Indeed, O'Laughlin writes, 'It is in relation to Merton's autobiographical works, especially in his classic *Seven Storey Mountain*, that Merton and Nouwen are most alike.'[34] Like Merton's *The Sign of Jonas*, Nouwen's *Genesee Diary* juxtaposes the 'mundane' with the 'transcendent.'[35] It is clearly influenced by the earlier work and records, perhaps subliminally at this stage, the realisation for Nouwen that he could live a spiritual life earthed in his studies in psychology without becoming a monk.

During those Yale years Nouwen met regularly with Donald P. McNeill and Douglas A. Morrison and together wrote *Compassion*.[36] It was a long time in its composition before being brought to press in 1981 and being published the following year. The typescript was rewritten several times as a result of feedback from many people who read it critically or used it in their own teaching.[37]

The increasing awareness of the radical nature of Christ's call to compassion shapes the three parts of the book. First, Nouwen and his co-authors write about the compassionate God, revealed in Jesus Christ, because it is God's own compassion that constitutes the basis and source of compassion. Secondly, they examine what it means to live a compassionate life as followers of Christ. Thirdly, and lastly, they explore the compassionate way of prayer and action, since it is through these two disciplines, which guide the relationships with oneself, God, and one's fellow human beings, that God's compassion can manifest itself in work, leisure, and prayer.

'Let the old "interested and interesting" self die and … receive a new self which is hidden in God'

In his Preface to the Japanese edition of *The Seven Storey Mountain*, published in 1968, that is, twenty years after the book's first publication in English,[38] Merton comments that so much had changed since the late 1940s, not least in his own response to the world. 'Since that time,' he confesses, 'I have learned, I believe, to look back into that world with greater compassion, seeing those in it not as alien to myself, not as peculiar and deluded strangers, but as identified with myself.'[39] Nouwen, himself, perceives that, 'In silence [Merton's] flight from people had become compassion for them.'[40] And this was to prove of tremendous importance to Nouwen.

> Although Merton was a much deeper thinker than Henri Nouwen, Thomas Merton exemplified for Nouwen the kind of awakened and inspired Christian writer who was fully engaged with his faith and reaching out to learn from and interact with the world.[41]

Nouwen perceives, 'It belonged to the essence of [Merton's] vocation to let the old "interested and interesting" self die and to receive a new self which is hidden in God.'[42]

Going further back in the life of Thomas Merton we find him by the end of December 1942, the twenty-six-year-old Thomas, arriving at the Abbey of Our Lady of Gethsemani, 'completely alone, with a small duffel bag in his hand.'[43] Nouwen at the time was ten years old, dressing up as a priest in his family home, and sharing his belief with his family and friends. At Gethsemani Merton lived as a member of the Trappist community until 1968, spending his last three years living in a hermitage within the grounds of the Abbey. Before entering the Abbey, Merton had given his clothes to the African Americans in Harlem, his books to the Franciscans and one of his friends, his diary, the manuscript of his novel *Journal of My Escape from the Nazis*, and his poetry to another friend with whom he had studied while at Columbia, the American poet Mark Van Doren (1894-1972), and he now offered his life to God. Such a difference to Nouwen, who was to arrive at L'Arche Daybreak with his large removal van crammed full of his clutter! This veritable caravanserai is, I think, one of the most symbolic scenes of Nouwen as he arrives at L'Arche with his baggage, his 'clutter', as we shall read.

In 1974 Nouwen was invited for a long stay at the Abbey of the Genesee. He had just been granted tenure at Yale after having taught there for three years. Although his long retreat at the newly founded monastery in New York showed Nouwen that he was not cut out for monastic isolation,[44] the ideals and vision of monastic spirituality informed much of his later thought. There were to be several other visits and another extended stay in 1979. But the very physical demands made on the Trappists – 'baking bread, sawing wood, hauling rocks'[45] – were almost more than Nouwen could bear and it was to be a different type of community wherein Nouwen was to ultimately find his earthly home. O'Laughlin concludes, 'Although he realized that he was not cut out for monastic isolation, *the ideals and vision of monastic spirituality informed all that he did from then on*.'[46] One has only to glance at the pages of *Pray to Live, Clowning in Rome*, or *The Way of the Heart* to discover the veracity of this statement. From their positions of enclosure, the one spiritual, the other physical, both Merton and Nouwen looked out upon a world engaged with problems of war and peace, civil rights, and Latin American injustice.

'Merton and Nouwen', as Fr John Eudes Bamberger recorded in an interview with Michael Ford, 'were very different types of people and they wrote to a different audience from different levels of experience … Henri was basically a teacher and a communicator on the popular level … Merton was basically a poet, a literary figure.' The miracle in reflecting on Merton and Nouwen, as indeed when reflecting on any of Nouwen's mentors, is the unique God-given personalities and gifts which each of them not only in the end accepted, but in truth owned and used in showing their compassionate responses to others. 'Both were deeply sensitive to the suffering of others,' writes Michael Ford in *Spiritual Masters for all Seasons*.[47]

Compassion includes confrontation and this includes confronting oneself, recognising the fact that each human being is unique, that representing oneself as a copy of one's hero is self- destructive, is not being true to oneself, and does not give any glory to God. Direct confrontation is 'a true expression of compassion … Compassion without confrontation fades quickly into fruitless sentimental commiseration.' However, 'if confrontation is to be an expression of patient action, it must be humble.' It is difficult to confront compassionately. Whenever confrontation is poisoned by the desire for attention, for power, or for revenge, it can so easily become self-serving and stop being compassionate. Confrontation, then, includes *self*-confrontation.[48]

This self-confrontation is brought home clearly in Merton's account of his 'Fourth and Walnut' experience[49] given in *Conjectures of a Guilty Bystander*.[50] He realised, experientially, his solidarity with the rest of the human race, and this realisation was, for him, liberating. 'It was like waking from a dream of separateness, of spurious self-isolation in a special world, the world of renunciation and supposed holiness,' Merton remarked. 'The whole illusion of a separate holy existence is a dream.' Merton was by no means questioning the reality of his vocation, or of his monastic life but he had come to realise that the idea of 'separation from the world' did not mean that monks were a different species of human being, types of 'pseudo-angels', that the monastic life was not of 'an order outside everyday existence in a contingent world', nor did it 'entitle one to despise the secular.'[51]

Merton unpacks what this difference is and describes the responsibility it brings. Not only those living a religious life but every human being belonged to God. 'We just happen to be conscious of it, and to make a profession out of this consciousness,' he wrote. But that by no means meant that monks were to consider themselves different, or even better, than others. 'The whole idea is preposterous.'[52]

Merton was now more fully awake – and free to love. And it is in his correspondence with the 'outside' world that Merton's feelings of solidarity grew. His growing feelings of compassion had taken root and were beginning to blossom.

This particular means of voluntary displacement, from achieving notable success in the world of academia to 'prayer centered around an immersion in the liturgy, individual growth as part of community, and oversight by an abbot or another monk who had made progress in the life of the Spirit,'[53] had deeply affected Nouwen. Merton had been proof that being a monk didn't necessarily prevent inquiry or writing. And, on the face of it, monasticism had appeared to Nouwen to provide structure and companionship. It had been a life that Nouwen explored and realised was not one to which he had been called. But at the heart of this monastic spirituality was the removal of self from the world in order to rest in God. Both Merton and Nouwen experienced very real struggles in dealing with the world's expectations of them. Nouwen, more than Merton, found removing himself from the world an ongoing challenge. Yet, both discovered, by resting in God, the love with which both were loved, and the love which they had for all others.

'In the intimacy with God we develop a greater intimacy with people'

In Louisville, at the corner of Fourth and Walnut, in the center of the shopping district, I was suddenly overwhelmed with the realization that I loved all those people, that they were mine and I theirs, that we could not be alien to one another even though we were total strangers ... though 'out of the world' [monks] are in the same world as everybody else, the world of the bomb, the world of race hatred, the world of technology, the world of mass media, big business, revolution and all the rest.'[54]

In this *Conjectures* account of his 'Fourth and Walnut' experience, Merton thrills to the reality of the Incarnation, and what this reality means:

It is a glorious destiny to be a member of the human race, though it is a race dedicated to many absurdities and one which makes many terrible mistakes: yet, with all that, God Himself gloried in becoming a member of the human race. A member of the human race! To think that such a commonplace realization should suddenly seem like news that one holds the winning ticket in a cosmic sweepstake.[55]

As Merton gives an account of his 'Fourth and Walnut' experience, he exalts in being 'a man among others.' 'I have the immense joy of being *man*, a member of a race,' he adds, 'in which God Himself became incarnate.'[56]

In *Reaching Out* Nouwen quotes Merton on his union with Jesus through the Incarnation:

The union of the Christian with Christ ... is a mystical union in which Christ himself becomes the source and principle of divine life in me. Christ Himself ... 'breathes' in me divinely in giving me His Spirit.[57]

And, a couple of years later, Nouwen himself comments on this in *The Living Reminder* (1977):

It is in the intimacy with God that we develop a greater intimacy with people and it is in the silence and solitude of prayer that we indeed can touch the heart of the human suffering to which we want to minister.[58]

Perhaps nowhere is Merton's influence on Nouwen better illustrated than in the latter's response to the 'Fourth and Walnut' epiphany. This experience of solidarity was of such a depth that both men were transfigured by it, at first and second hand. For Nouwen it was a revelatory moment that would continue to influence his own thinking about the relationships between contemplation and action, withdrawal and compassion, catalysing his desire for inclusivity and unity.

The significance of Christ's Incarnation *vis á vis* compassion is unpacked in *Compassion*. By calling God 'Immanuel', by understanding with both our heart and mind the words at the opening of John's Gospel, 'the Word became flesh and lived among us' (Jn 1: 14), 'we recognize God has committed himself to live in solidarity with us, to share our joys and pains, to defend and protect us, and to suffer all of life with us.'[59] We recognise that God is a 'close' God, 'our refuge', 'our stronghold', 'our wisdom', 'our helper', 'our shepherd', 'our love'. And it is in this 'divine solidarity', this 'most intimate solidarity', that God's compassion is anchored. This is a solidarity 'that allows us to say with the psalmist, "This is our God, and we are the people he pastures, the flock that he guides"' (Ps 95:7).[60] And there is no sense in which God is in solidarity on an individualistic level. Rather, God is in solidarity with all, irrespective of background or status.

The three writers of *Compassion* earth what they have written by stating that this becomes known 'because in Jesus, God's compassion became visible to us.'[61] 'He was the concrete embodiment of this divine compassion in our world ... Jesus' response to ... all those who came to him with their suffering, flowed from the divine compassion which led God to become one of us.'[62] 'What is important here is not the cure of the sick, but the deep compassion that moved Jesus to these cures.'[63] 'He did not cure to prove, to impress, or to convince. His cures were the natural expression of his being our God ... The great mystery is not the cures, but the infinite compassion which is their source ... They witness to the infinite fecundity of his divine compassion, and show us the beautiful fruits of his solidarity with our condition.'[64]

Nouwen continued to reflect on this in *In the House of the Lord* where, in a chapter headed 'Fecundity and Love', there is a passage that describes the way of God. 'The way of God', Nouwen begins, 'is the way of weakness. The great news of the Gospel is precisely that God became small and vulnerable, and hence bore fruit among us.' Nouwen continues,

> The most fruitful life ever lived is the life of Jesus, who did not cling to his divine power but became as we are (see Phil 2:6-7). Jesus brought us new life in ultimate vulnerability. He came to us as a small child, dependent on the care and protection of others. He lived for us as a poor preacher, without any political, economic, or military power. He died for us nailed on a cross as a useless criminal. It is in this extreme vulnerability that our salvation was won. The fruit of this poor and failing existence is eternal life for all who believe in him.

Then Nouwen focuses on how humanity might be aware of this vulnerability. 'It is very hard for us to grasp even a little bit of the mystery of God's vulnerability,' he remarks,

> Yet, when we have eyes to see and ears to hear we can see it in so many ways and in many places. We can see it when a child is born, the fruit of the love of two people who came together without defences and embraced each other in weakness. We can see it in the graceful smiles of poor people and in the warm affection of the handicapped. We can see it every time people ask forgiveness and are reconciled.[65]

This compassion is obviously quite different from 'superficial or passing feelings of sorrow or sympathy.'[66] Nouwen and his co-authors point out that there is a beautiful expression used on a dozen occasions in the Gospels, which is 'to be moved with compassion.' The Greek verb *splangchnizomai* is used on each occasion. Jesus' *splangchna* or entrails, his guts, 'the place where our most intimate and intense emotions are located,'[67] are stirred.[68]

'Compassion', Beumer comments in his biography of Nouwen, 'can be seen as a moral designation that helps humanity along.'[69] 'Who would not feel compassion for a poor old man, a hungry child, a paralyzed soldier, a fearful girl?'[70] Nouwen and his two co-authors ask. 'Indeed', they continue, 'We immediately identify being compassionate with being human.'[71] 'But, if being human and being compassionate are the same,' they continue, 'then why is humanity torn by conflict, war, hatred, and oppression?'[72]

The word compassion is derived from the Latin words *pati* and *cum*, which together mean 'to suffer with.' When compassion is looked at in this sense, then, it soon becomes evident that something more is involved than a general kindness or tender-heartedness.

'Compassion', the authors argue, 'is not among our most natural responses … it is not as natural a phenomenon as it might first appear.'[73] 'We as human beings are not all that eager to enter into the brokenness of this world,' writes Beumer. 'On the contrary, we would much rather keep our distance.'[74] It is precisely this ambiguous place of compassion that provides both the reason for this book and its starting point. 'How can people be compassionate when their natural inclination is to shrink from and run away from compassion?' enquires Beumer.[75] *Compassion* points towards an answer.

Christians may say with Paul, 'I live now not with my own life but with the life of Christ who lives in me' (Gal 2:20).[76] Through this union Christians may be raised out of their competitiveness and rivalries and enter into a different relationship with God, with others, and with themselves, a way of life lived by the Apostles and 'those great Christians who have witnessed for Christ through the centuries.'[77]

Merton's 'voluntary displacement',[78] and resting in God, paradoxically although seeming to separate Merton from the world, actually enabled him to discover a deeper union with it. In his Foreword to *Merton's Palace of Nowhere* Nouwen acknowledged that:

> I would realize that Merton was and is no more than a window through whom we may perhaps catch a glimpse of the One who had called him to a life of prayer and solitude. Every attempt to put Merton on a pedestal would not only horrify Merton himself, but would also be in direct contrast to everything for which he stood.[79]

Nouwen was to return to these concepts of separation and unity a few years later in *The Way of the Heart* when he places Merton in the long tradition of desert fathers from Anthony of Egypt onwards who, in their centring on Jesus, enabled them to offer those in the world a more hopeful *stasis*:

> They knew that they were helpless to do any good for others as long as they floundered about in the wreckage. But once they got a foothold on solid ground, things were different. Then they had not only the power but even the obligation to pull the whole world to safety after them.[80]
>
> It is in this solitude that we become compassionate people, deeply aware of our solidarity in brokenness with all of humanity and ready to reach out to anyone in need.[81]

'Voluntary displacement', Nouwen was again to write some years later,[82] 'leads to compassionate living precisely because it moves us from positions of distinction to positions of sameness, from being in special places to being everywhere.' In a word, voluntary displacement leads to the acceptance of Christ, not self, being at the centre of one's life, a concept that would take root and grow in Nouwen to the end of his life.

Following Christ, mirroring his divine compassion as far as it is able, brings us into a different state of being. Nouwen expresses this beautifully in a handout used in his Introduction to Spirituality course at Harvard:

> [Jesus] lives his life out in such an intimate solidarity with us that we can say that he is more fully alive than any other human being. It is through this human 'sameness' that we can come to share in his divine life.[83]

Merton himself, after some twenty years of monastic life, was to write in his Preface to the Japanese edition of *The Seven Storey Mountain*, 'My monastery is not a home. It is not a place where I am rooted and established on the earth. It is not an environment in which I become aware of myself as an individual, but rather a place in which I disappear from the world as an object of interest in order to be everywhere in it by hiddenness and compassion.'[84]

It is worth remarking, I think, that McNeill, Morrison, and Nouwen were all tempted from time to time to drop the writing of this book and try something less challenging instead. They recognised the fact both individually and collectively that whenever they faced this temptation, they were doubting the value of a commitment to Christ. As the call to compassion grew, the thought of ignoring this call seemed increasingly to be a refusal to directly face the radical challenge of the Christian faith. Towards the end of their introduction, they write:

> We have become less optimistic and, hopefully, more realistic. National and international events, deeper study of the Scriptures, and the many critical responses of friends, have made us less confident about our 'compassionate tendencies' and more aware of the radical quality of Jesus' command to be compassionate as your loving God is compassionate.[85]

As the book unfolds, the command penetrates to the very root of human life.

'Thank God, thank God, that I am like other men, that I am only a man among others'

In Nouwen's sermon preached at St Paul's Church, Columbia University, New York City, in December 1978 – the tenth anniversary of Thomas Merton's death – he reflects on the Second Letter of Peter, in particular on waiting actively for God's coming, and says God's promise of his coming 'is not hanging above us in the air, but is deeply embedded in our everyday life.' He argues that no one in our day has understood this so well, or articulated this so clearly, as Thomas Merton. 'For Merton', Nouwen continues, 'contemplation and action can never be separated.'

> All of Merton's writings on social action make the same point: as long as you act to prove yourself, to justify yourself, or to get rid of your guilt-feelings, you will quickly lose heart and do more harm than good.

In *Reaching Out* Nouwen comments, 'As his life grew in spiritual maturity, Merton came to see with a penetrating clarity that solitude did not separate him from his contemporaries but instead brought him into a deep communion with them.'[86]

Looking at the work of Saint Peter and Saint Paul, Teresa of Ávila, Martin Luther King Jr, and Mother Teresa, Nouwen writes that none of these ever tried to solve the world's problems, or sought to receive praise or prizes, but, *kenotically* freed from their own compulsions, they responded spontaneously 'to the experience of God's active presence in their lives.'

'Here', Nouwen concludes:

> We touch the core of Merton's life and work. It is the Eucharist, the eternal act of thanks given by Christ to his Father, an act of thanksgiving in which we become participants. Merton's life as a Christian, a monk, and a priest was anchored in the Eucharist. What really counted for him was not his books and articles, his name and fame, but the Lord Jesus Christ who came to make all of life a Eucharist. For in the Eucharist, all is God's action ... With Peter [Merton] asked, 'What kind of people must we be?' And to this he answered, 'We must be holy in our conduct and devotion, looking in contemplation for the coming of the Lord and trying to hasten it by acts of repentance and gratitude.'[87]

'Prayer and action can never be seen as contradictory or mutually exclusive. Prayer without action grows into powerless pietism, and action without prayer degenerates into questionable manipulation.'[88] Nouwen and his co-writers point out that 'our actions, like our prayers, must be a manifestation of God's compassionate presence in the midst of our world.' Praying leading into action can result in patient actions, 'through which the healing, consoling, comforting, reconciling, and unifying love of God can touch the heart of humanity.' Action as a consequence of compassionate prayer 'requires the willingness to respond to the very concrete needs of the moment.'[89]

The importance of gifts, especially the awareness of each other's gifts, enables a letting go of obsession. This new way of non-competitiveness enables compassion. People open their eyes to each other. Living in this way, in solidarity with each other, we are enabled to recognise each other's gifts. Our unique talents are no longer objects of competition but gifts that unite the community. 'With increasing clarity, we can see the beauty in each other and call it forth so that it may become a part of our total life together ... Community, as a new way of being together, leads to the discovery or rediscovery of each other's hidden talents and makes us realize our own unique contribution to the common life.'[90] As these unique talents are recognised in each other, people also learn to let go of the obsession with their own. In paying attention to each other, they begin to recognise their own value, and this 'simple experience of being valuable and important to someone else has a tremendous re-creative power.'[91] Merton invites each one of us to an ever-deepening awareness of the presence of God. 'He continually unmasks the illusions that we know God and so frees us to see the Lord in always new and surprising ways.'[92] 'Where people have entered into the mind of Christ and no longer think of their own interests first, the compassionate Lord manifests himself and offers his healing presence to all who turn to him.'[93] 'It is this inner solidarity,' writes Nouwen in *Reaching Out*, 'which prevents self-righteousness and makes compassion possible.'

Commenting on this openness or increased awareness to the presence of God in the world, in each one of us, in every created thing, O'Laughlin adds:

> Becoming free to see things in 'new and surprising ways' was central to the vocations of Thomas Merton, Vincent van Gogh, and Henri Nouwen, and the type of 'seeing' they practised proceeds from a similar kind of contemplative and artistic engagement. This creative process leads to a deeper comprehension of aspects of the world that are normally hidden or unnoticed … Vincent van Gogh, Thomas Merton, and Henri Nouwen were not looking beyond this world in search of some heavenly realm. All three were seeking God's presence in the world around us.[94]

Merton's 'very deep and intimate' relation with other persons and Nouwen's response are so important and pertinent that they deserve to be given in full. Merton posits:

> Once God has called you to solitude, everything you touch leads you further into solitude … What is my new desert? The name of it is *compassion*. There is no wilderness so terrible, so beautiful, so arid and so fruitful as the wilderness of compassion. It is the only desert that shall truly flourish like the lily. It shall become a pool, it shall bud forth and blossom and rejoice with joy. It is in the desert of compassion that the thirsty land turns into springs of water, that the poor possess all things.[95]

Nouwen responds:

> Perhaps most moving in *The Sign of Jonas* is the development of compassion in solitude. In silence Merton discovered humanity once again. The new name for the desert in which he saw many of his self-constructed ambitions destroyed was: *compassion*. He learned to feel and respect silence in the life of another. He learned there to love his

monastic brothers, not for what they say but for what they are. He saw now, with amazement, the quietude and solitude that lived in them. Now he wanted only to be a man among people, a member of humanity.[96]

This realisation, borne (not unlike John the Baptist) of that purity of heart that continuously points away from self and towards the divine, enabled Merton to let go of his preoccupations with himself in order to touch the world 'with the hand of compassion.'[97] In this solitude that generated compassion, concludes Nouwen, curiosity was transfigured into admiration, direction into guidance, silence into a place where 'all can really be together in God.'[98] Early on, Nouwen realised the paradox that Merton was living out:

> The paradox of Merton's life indeed is that his withdrawal from the world brought him into closer contact with it. The more he was able to convert his restless loneliness into a solitude of heart, the more he could discover the pains of his world in his own inner centre and respond to them. His compassionate solidarity with the human struggle made him a spokesman for many who, although lacking in his talent for writing, shared his solitude.[99]

Merton, in his 'earthiness', in his complete absence of pretension, in a word, in his utter transparency, was 'a good guide', 'a perceptive observer', 'able to articulate his outer and inner worlds in such a way that his fellow travellers discovered in him an excellent interpreter of their own experiences and a good friend to help them find the way through often unknown territory' – a territory that detaches us from our 'false, illusory self – a self that is little more than the collective evaluations and affirmations of our surroundings – and opens us up 'to receive a new self that is participation in the life of God.'[100]

O'Laughlin writes in *God's Beloved*, 'Merton, like Van Gogh, epitomized for Henri a kind of engaged contemplation of God in what can be seen before us.'[101] While Merton himself reflects in *New Seeds of Contemplation*:

> Contemplation is beyond aesthetic intuition, beyond art, beyond poetry … It knows God by seeming to touch Him. Or rather it knows Him as if it had been invisibly touched by Him … Touched by Him who has no hands, but who is pure Reality and the source of all that is real! Hence, contemplation is a sudden gift of awareness, an awakening to the Real within all that is real.[102]

It is through contemplation that Merton, and later Nouwen, became, to use Julian of Norwich's phrase, 'one-ed to God' and thus one-ed to the whole of creation.[103]

In his solitude Merton had discovered the possibility of a compassion that was essentially non-violent (in marked contrast to the violence being exhibited in America during the 1950s and 1960s), and this nonviolence to be 'the inherent quality of spiritual unity.'[104] Nouwen goes on to write in Chapter 4 of *Pray to Live*, 'The creative spirit of unity that one can find in the silence of one's own heart is not a strictly personal possession, but the life of the spirit of all men and women.'[105] 'Here,' Nouwen remarks towards the end of the fourth chapter, 'we have come back to the compassion that must be formed in one's heart, a compassion that comes out of a deep experience of solidarity.'[106] As will soon be discovered, this compassion was to be both the key and means of reaching out where the individual stands alongside his neighbour before God in a psycho-therapeutic way. Michael Ford writes in his *Spiritual Masters for All Seasons*, 'Merton ... had lived the very solitude of which he had written, a solitude that had led him, not only into his own heart, but also into the heart of every person with whom he was one in Christ.'[107]

Returning to the subject of Merton's Fourth and Walnut experience, after his paean of praise for being a man among men, Merton emphasizes the importance of solitude:

> This changes nothing in the sense and value of my solitude, for it is in fact the function of solitude to make one realize such things with a clarity that would be impossible to anyone completely immersed in the other cares, the other illusions, and all the automatisms of a tightly collective existence.

Then Merton makes an extraordinary statement regarding solitude which offers his readers a deeper understanding and appreciation of that solitude:

> My solitude, however, is not my own, for I see now how much it belongs to them – and that I have a responsibility for it in their regard, not just in my own. It is because I am one with them that I owe it to them to be alone, and when I am alone they are not 'they' but my own self. There are no strangers![108]

In this solitude, Merton's solitude that is also theirs, he comes to a deeper realisation that each one is unique:

> Then it was as if I suddenly saw the secret beauty of their hearts, the depths of their hearts where neither sin nor desire nor self-knowledge

can reach, the core of their reality, the person that each one is in God's eyes. If only they could all see themselves as they really *are*. If only we could see each other that way all the time. There would be no more war, no more hatred, no more cruelty, no more greed ... I suppose the big problem would be that we would fall down and worship each other. But this cannot be *seen*, only believed and 'understood' by a peculiar gift.[109]

As we have found, Merton and Nouwen shared many similarities, but in spite of these clear parallels, they were, essentially, unalike. Malcolm Higgins lists their similarities in his *Genius Born of Anguish: The Life and Legacy of Henri Nouwen*.[110] They were both children of the twentieth century, absorbed by psychology and psychiatry in addition to being clinically depressed at one stage in their respective lives; they both experienced struggles in relation to sexuality; both experienced the 'dynamic' and 'tension' between solitude and community;[111] developed an all-pervasive and controversial 'spirituality of peace-making'; feared 'the soul-destroying power of the cult of celebrity at the same time as it held them in its thrall;' remained 'quintessentially self-disclosing;' – and they both experienced 'at its core the exacting demands of compassion in a time of dissolution – personal, social, and ecclesial.'

In a chapter headed 'Pilgrims of Wisdom and Peace' Higgins notes, 'to some degree they spoke out of similar contexts. To some degree they addressed similar crises.'[112] However, Higgins clearly points out, Merton and Nouwen were very much their own men.

> Merton and Nouwen were also starkly unlike, and it is too grandiose and simplistic to see them as easy replications of each other. Bamberger, in particular, in an oral interview he gave biographer Michael Ford, is especially keen on differentiating them, given his own privileged point of access to both:
>
> 'Merton was my spiritual director and my teacher, and I worked with him for ten years, so I knew his style very well. Henri's style was very different from Merton's. I think Merton was an unusual type of person; I don't think Henri was.'[113]

In the same interview Bamberger tersely remarks, 'Anybody who thinks Nouwen was the Merton of his generation either didn't know Henri or didn't know Merton.'

If, then, we are to be Christ-like, it is essential that we constantly claim our true identity, 'that we are God's children, the beloved sons and daughters of our heavenly Father ... not because we have proven ourselves worthy of God's love, but because God freely chose us.'[114] At times, Christians are called and enabled to be 'Christ' for others. In perceiving the presence of Christ in themselves and each another, through discerning the gifts of the Spirit, Christians come to the realisation that more is shared in common than was first thought. Such a realisation can enable a sharing in the divine life. It is at this point that the commonality of being sons and daughters of God, brothers and sisters of one another, is realised.

And, developing out of this, it is important, too, that we, in Merton's words, 'guard the image of man for it is the image of God.'[115] The tragedy is, of course, that our capacity to perceive the divine image, in ourselves and in others, is so frequently obscured. Worse, as Merton writes in *The New Man* (1961), 'the fact that we are all united to God in one natural image and in one human nature ... cannot ... keep [us] ... from destroying in one another the very image of Him [we] ought to love above all things.'[116] Being Christ-*like*, loving with a pure heart is and can always and only be partial and incomplete. However, this lack of completeness did not diminish the quality of the decisions made by the Second Vatican Council, or their urgency. To be a responsible Christian engaging with an increasingly fractured world meant walking together, respecting the other, sharing responsibility together for the common good. As *Sollicitudo Rei Socialis* (John Paul II, 1987) was to have it, walking alongside is 'a firm and persevering determination' to commit oneself 'to the common good; that is to say to the good of all and of each individual because we are all really responsible for all.'[117] For Nouwen,[118] as for Merton,[119] *every* Christian is a pilgrim on the road to Emmaus.

The very proximity of Christ, however, can prevent us, like the two disciples, from recognising him. When we see Christ face to face, we are blinded by that light. We fail to see the uniqueness of every person illuminated by that same light.

As Christopher Pramuk ponders in *Sophia*, as images of the divine, we are invited to 'an all-encompassing Christian inclusivism, the ground for an openness and dialogue that positively expects to encounter Christ ... hidden in the stranger.'[120] Part of that invitation is the participating in God's compassion, Christ-like discipleship, reaching out to all people, at all times, and in all places, with the heart of God.

Nouwen records Merton's relief and joy on his discovery of 'sameness' and then goes on to make manifest the significance of this discovery:

> When Thomas Merton came to the existential realization of this solidarity, he cried out: 'This sense of liberation of an illusory difference was such a relief and such a joy to me that I almost laughed out loud. And I suppose my happiness could have taken form in these words: 'Thank God, thank God, that I am like other men, that I am only a man

among others ... It is a glorious destiny to be a member of the human race.' The important point for Merton is not the recognition that we are not so much different from other people, but the fact that the full affirmation of our sameness reveals our deepest sense of self. What counts, therefore, is not just accepting that we are the same as others but desiring to participate in this human sameness as fully and deeply as possible.[121]

At the end of the *Conjectures* account of the 'Fourth and Walnut' experience there is a very fine passage concerning *le point vierge*, the very 'kernel' of one's being, 'the embryo of the eternal child eternally present within each person'[122] which unpacks some of Merton's thinking on our dependence and relationship as children of God:

> Again, that expression, *le point vierge*, (I cannot translate it) comes in here. At the center of our being is a point of nothingness which is untouched by sin and by illusion, a point of pure truth, a point or spark which belongs entirely to God, which is never at our disposal, from which God disposes of our lives, which is inaccessible to the fantasies of our own mind or the brutalities of our own will. This little point of nothingness and of *absolute poverty* is the pure glory of God in us. It is so to speak His name written in us, as our poverty, as our indigence, as our dependence, as our sonship. It is like a pure diamond, blazing with the invisible light of heaven. It is in everybody, and if we could see it we would see these billions of points of light coming together in the face and blaze of a sun that would make all the darkness and cruelty of life vanish completely ... I have no program for this seeing. It is only given. But the gate of heaven is everywhere.[123]

This manner of seeing, and then seeing more deeply, should not really surprise us. After all, Nouwen reminds us elsewhere, hadn't the two disciples on their way to Emmaus in eating bread together recognised Jesus together with them and *then* experienced a new relationship between each other?

Responding to God's call to follow Jesus, leaving the ordinary places, Christians discover one another as fellow travellers, making manifest God's compassion in the world from day to day, as the three co-writers of *Compassion* discuss in a chapter headed 'Togetherness'. The Acts of the Apostles presents a glimpse of the togetherness experienced by the first converts and to be experienced again by people in the twenty-first century. 'The faithful all lived together and owned everything in common ... day by day the Lord added to their community <literally, their togetherness> those destined to be saved' (2:44-47). Voluntary displacement, then, is not an end in itself but a means to gathering everyone together in a new way. Another caveat is delivered. No form of displacement is authentic unless it brings people closer together. If people displace themselves in order to become in any way outstanding, or special, or unique they are simply and only displaying subtle forms of competitiveness that lead to elitism and not community.

As Higgins writes in *Genius Born of Anguish*, Nouwen 'came to understand near the end of his life that the wounded-ness of others, as well as his own wounded-ness, were not simply existential realities to be recorded, analysed, probed, and exorcized, *but* a summons to intense and authentic living.'[124] In the next chapter we discover how Nouwen began to transfigure these gaping wounds into gateways of possibility.

> *He came to appreciate in time that his wounds were not so much*
> *'gaping abysses' but 'gateways to new life,' and that these very gateways*
> *constitute a spiritual cartography of their own: they define the terrain,*
> *the hills and valleys, contours and lineaments, of a psychological and*
> *emotional life aching into holiness.*[125]

Chapter 2

Vincent van Gogh, Henri Nouwen's wounded healer

I experienced connections between Vincent's struggle and my own, and realized more and more that Vincent was becoming my wounded healer. He painted what I had not before dared to look at; he questioned what I had not before dared to speak about; and he entered into the spaces of my heart that I had not dared to come close to. By so doing he brought me in touch with many of my fears and gave me the courage to go further and deeper in my search for a God who loves.[1]

One of the most profound themes, and one of the most consistent, that run through Henri Nouwen's life, one of the *leitmotifs*, is that of the wounded healer. Not only did Henri see himself as a wounded healer but it is obvious from the quotation at the head of our chapter that he found in Vincent van Gogh (1853-90) someone who was becoming Nouwen's very own wounded healer. Van Gogh was a kindred spirit, a spiritual brother, whose own brokenness and suffering was to prove an astonishing source from which the artist drew on to create his extraordinary corpus of work, and from which Nouwen also drew on to be increasingly in touch with himself and others, to be a channel through whom others could experience the touch of the Holy Spirit, to be compassionate.

Although Nouwen perceived the works of a number of painters as a means of communicating with the Creator God, notably, Cezanne and Rodin, it was the influence of two fellow countrymen that was to be of supreme importance in his life – Vincent van Gogh and Rembrandt van Rijn. Van Gogh admired Rembrandt, writing frequently and at length about him in his letters, and, together, they exercised, in their own different ways, a deep and lasting influence on Nouwen's spiritual journey towards, as Nouwen himself puts it, 'a God who loves.'

In a strikingly similar way to Van Gogh, Nouwen was able to get under the skin of those whom he came alongside. Michael W. Higgins, in his *Genius Born of Anguish*, has remarked that Nouwen deployed his own phenomenological approach, 'of inserting himself into the experience of others, of attending to the living human documents in a way that brought into a creative symbiosis the psychological needs and the spiritual needs of his clients.'[2] And, although Nouwen had written his seminal work, *The Wounded Healer: Ministry in Contemporary Society* back in 1972, here he was, almost a couple of decades later, describing Van Gogh becoming his own wounded healer and guide.

What did Nouwen mean by the phrase 'wounded healer'? Michael Ford writes:

> Over the course of more than 20 years, [Nouwen] was responsible for popularising the concept of the wounded healer which he traced back to its biblical foundations. His work transformed pastoral teaching in the Church by showing that priests and ministers need not be afraid to own their own wounds and use them to heal others. But the struggles had to be lived through in the heart, not merely discussed in the mind. The healing had to come from the sacred centre, that place of divine encounter which resourced so much of his theology and teaching.[3]

It was not Nouwen's own phrase but one that he came across in his training in psychology. It was, in fact, Carl Jung who wrote in his autobiographical *Memories, Dreams and Reflections*, published in the early 1960s, 'The doctor is effective only when he himself is affected [by the patient]. "Only the wounded physician heals." But when the doctor wears his personality like a coat of armour, he has no effect.'[4] There is a clear parallel here with the writing of Peter Naus, a Dutch graduate in social psychology who had known Nouwen at Nijmegen and had spent a year teaching as a visiting professor with him at Notre Dame, who comments:

> Henri's books almost all start with human experience to which he gives a spiritual meaning. His core concept, the wounded healer, is a very profound spiritual concept – but it's also a very profound psychological concept within a phenomenological, not a behaviourist, tradition ... Henri found a way of connecting the psychological with the transcendental approach, so he would say to pastoral people, 'Do not stay at the psychological level, you have to bring something else, you have to clarify the transcendental dimension. As a pastoral counsellor

you have to show how human experience can be elucidated by reference to the Gospel.'[5]

What are the biblical foundations for the phrase 'wounded healer' that Ford refers to in his book, *Wounded Prophet*? There is a tractate Sanhedrin, in the Seder Nezikin section of the Talmud, which makes the same point. In response to the question, 'How shall I know [the Messiah]?' Rabbi Yoshua ben Levi is told by Elijah the prophet,

> He is sitting among the poor covered with wounds. The others unbind all their wounds at the same time and then bind them up again. But he unbinds one at a time and binds it up again, saying to himself: 'Perhaps I shall be needed: if so I must always be ready so as not to delay for a moment.'[6]

Nouwen explained that Jesus gave this tractate a deeper significance and a fuller interpretation by making his own broken body the means to liberation and new life. Similarly, priests and ministers were called not only to care for others but to make their own wounds an important source of healing. And the wounds he most often talked of were those of alienation, isolation, loneliness, and separation.[7]

In the final chapter of *The Wounded Healer* Nouwen describes hospitality as 'a central attitude of the minister *of whichever persuasion* who wants to make his own wounded condition available to others as a source of healing … This hospitality', continues Nouwen, 'requires that the minister know where he stands and whom he stands for, but it also requires that he allow others to enter his life, come close to him and ask him how their lives connect with his.'

> Nobody can predict where this will lead us, because every time a host allows himself to be influenced by his guest he takes a risk not knowing how they will affect his life. But it is exactly in common searches and shared risks that new ideas are born, that new visions reveal themselves and that new roads become visible.
>
> We do not know where we will be two, ten or twenty years from now. What we can know, however, is that man suffers and that a sharing of suffering can make us move forward.

Nouwen ends *The Wounded Healer* with the words:

> The minister is called to make this forward thrust credible to his many guests, so that they do not stay but have a growing desire to move on, in the conviction that the full liberation of man and his world is still to come.[8]

The Wounded Healer was an instant success. In it Nouwen compares the wound of loneliness to the Grand Canyon: 'a deep incision in the surface of our existence which has become an inexhaustible source of beauty and understanding.'[9] He goes on to write about ministers who are called not only to care for other people's wounds but also to transfigure their own wounds into a beneficial source of healing. Many seminaries and churches used the work as a textbook for ministry and it has been regarded by some as a 'modern classic'.[10]

However, the *Wounded Healer* was not well received by everyone. The Christian commentator, John McFarland, comments:

> Many people see the Nouwen minister as a weakling and either turn away in disgust, suspect they are being used by the minister, or treat the pastor like a bumbling grandchild. The wounded-healer pastor may become an inward-looking chaplain of the emotions who forgets her or his function as a prophet of God and servant of those in need.[11]

Additionally, a few criticised the concept of the wounded healer, misinterpreting Nouwen in their belief that he was calling for the removal of all distinctions between care-givers and those they serve. What Nouwen, in fact, was arguing for was that ministers, irrespective of denomination, should 'simply remain grounded in their own vulnerability, their brokenness in Christ, and resist the temptation to objectify their fellow Christians, making them into mere 'parishioners', 'clients', or 'directees'.'[12] Deeply rooted in the Clinical Pastoral Education movement, 'the concept of the utilization of the self in ministry has become fully ensconced in the field of pastoral care.'[13] Nouwen skilfully modelled this concept by capitalising on the image of the 'wounded healer' as his guiding image. 'To be a healing, Christ-like presence for others, care-givers must be available as whole persons who participate simultaneously as both givers and receivers.'[14] In short, the Christian is called to be both 'the wounded minister' and 'the healing minister'.

In his doctoral thesis *An Exploration and Adaptation of Anton T. Boisen's Notion of the Psychiatric Chaplain in Responding to Current Issues in Clinical Chaplaincy*, Christopher E. De Bono is correct when he cautions that there is a danger over making a connection too simplistically or too directly when considering who the wounded healer is.[15] Later, De Bono adds, Nouwen warned his readers not to treat the 'wounded healer' image as a 'complete model' but suggested that it was, at most, 'his attempt to say something – not everything – about ministry.' He even goes so far as to suggest that:

> It was a kind of corrective to the effects of his own training: 'When I wrote about the minister as wounded healer I had recently acquired

academic degrees in both psychology and theology. After so much professional training I needed to remind myself that beyond all professionalism, ministry calls me to lay down my life for my friends and to make my own most personal experience with God available to others as a source of healing.[16]

I have referred to Peter Naus, Nouwen's Dutch friend from his Nijmegen days, who taught with Nouwen at Notre Dame, before moving on to St Jerome's University, Waterloo, Ontario (where he taught psychology from 1973 until his retirement in 1996). *Out of Solitude: Three Meditations of the Christian Life* is dedicated to Peter and his wife, Anke. The book, based on Mark 1:35 – Jesus withdrawing to a solitary place – grew out of three sermons Nouwen preached at Battell, the United Church of Christ at Yale. His thinking about solitude, sown in this book, blossomed in his later writings to form an important part of his spirituality.

One of the chapters of *Out of Solitude* focuses on waiting which solitude and contemplation engender and out of which healing may come:

> This intimate experience [of waiting with faith in God for his promises to be fulfilled, especially during times of discouragement or sorrow] in which every bit of life is touched by a bit of death can point us beyond the limits of our existence ... allowing our weeping and wailing to become the purifying preparation by which we are made ready to receive the joy that is promised to us.[17]

This comes close to a letter of Van Gogh to his brother, Theo, who, expressing the discipline of patient prayer, writes:

> There may be a great fire in our soul, yet no one ever comes to warm himself at it, and the passers-by only see a wisp of smoke coming through the chimney, and go along their way. Look here, now, what must be done? Must one tend the inner fire, have salt in oneself, wait patiently yet with how much impatience for the hour when somebody will come and sit down near it – maybe to stay? Let him who believes in God wait for the hour that will come sooner or later.[18]

'Patience', Nouwen and his two co-writers of *Compassion* argue, 'is the hard but fruitful discipline of the disciple of the compassionate God.'[19] When human beings are challenged they usually choose between two options, fighting or fleeing from the challenge. Patience, the authors suggest, is the third option. Patience, though, goes against the grain of natural impulses and because it counteracts the reflective impulse it is an extremely difficult discipline. Yet in the New Testament Jesus and Paul have much to say about patience. 'Patience is the quality of those who are the rich soil in which the seed can produce "its crop a hundredfold." "These are people," Jesus says, "with a noble and generous heart who have heard the word and take it to themselves and yield a harvest through their perseverance (*hypomonē*)"' (Lk 8:8, 15).[20] It is a quality by which Jesus sets great store. "By your endurance (*hypomonē*) you will gain your souls" (Lk 21:16-19). Paul exhorts his friend Timothy to be patient and gentle (1 Tm 6:11) and writes to the Colossians, 'You should be clothed in sincere compassion, in kindness and humility, gentleness and patience' (Col 3:12). It is in Paul's letter to the Romans that he most eloquently and thoroughly states that through patience Christians are living signs of God's compassionate love:

> We can boast about our sufferings. These sufferings bring patience, as we know, and patience brings perseverance, and perseverance brings hope, and this hope is not deceptive, because the love of God has been poured into our hearts by the Holy Spirit which has been given us. (Rm 5:3-5)

James picks up this conviction when he writes:

> Remember it is those who had endurance (*hypomeinantas*) that we say are the blessed ones. You have heard of the patience (*hypomonē*) of Job, and understood the Lord's purpose, realising that the Lord is kind and compassionate. (Jm 5:10-11)

'Thus, the New Testament presents the discipline of patience as the way to a life of discipleship which makes us living signs of God's compassionate presence in this world.'[21]

Patience opens people, the writers suggest, to a new experience of time.[22] Clock time seems always to make people leave an action or situation, breeding impatience and preventing any sense of compassionately being together.[23] On the other hand, patience 'dispels clock time and reveals a new time, the time of salvation ... the time lived from within and experienced as full time.'[24] The great events of the Gospels occur 'in the fullness of time.' Elizabeth bore her son John (Lk 1:57). Mary bore Jesus (Lk 2:6). Joseph and Mary brought Jesus to Jerusalem (Lk 2:22). All in the fullness of time. The way in which the Evangelists record events occurring, too, shows that they happened not in man's time, that is to say in 'clock time', but in the divine time of maturation. It happened that Zacharias was the priest to serve in the temple (Lk 1:5). It happened that they came together to circumcise John (Lk 1:59). It happened that a decree was issued by Caesar Augustus (Lk 2:1). It happened that Mary's time was full to have a child (Lk 2:6). All these happenings are described as moments of grace and salvation and we see that God's advent is recognised as the event of the fullness of time. Mark records Jesus' proclamation that the time had come to its fullness and that God's kingdom was close at hand (1:15). Paul, too, describes the great news in his letter to the Galatians 'When the time had come to its fullness God sent the Son, born of a woman ... so that we might receive adoption as children' (4:4-5). 'It is this full time, pregnant with new life,' McNeill, Morrison, and Nouwen conclude, 'that can be found through the discipline of patience ... Patience, thus, is the compassionate way that leads to the compassionate life.'[25]

Compassion, Nouwen points out earlier in *Out of Solitude*,[26] is required of all of us who live in relationship to God. Yet, he also points out, in our self-absorbed lives, Christians do not have the space left to listen to others, or allow them to come close. Only those who practise solitude will be able to be compassionate because solitude enables rest, centring, and *kenosis*. It also offers the quietness from which to hear God's voice that calls Christians, all Christians, to 'this radical lifestyle of compassion.'[27]

'He is a man who really struggled with real spiritual questions'

In 1968 Henri Nouwen left the Psychology Department at Notre Dame and travelled home to the Netherlands, teaching in Amsterdam and Utrecht (1968-70). He failed his doctoral thesis but received a second *doctorandus* on 7 October 1971, at Nijmegen, and returned to the States in order to teach pastoral theology at Yale (1971-81). It was a returning that was to lead to a discovery which, halfway through the decade, was to have an almost overwhelmingly spiritual impact on Nouwen.[28] In the mid-1970s Nouwen made a start in his studies of Van Gogh which was to make a profound impact on his understanding of compassion. Nouwen visited the Kröller-Möller Museum in the Netherlands, spending hours looking at Van Gogh's paintings and drawings, and in private he spent time reading and re-reading 900 of Van Gogh's letters, 650 of which are addressed to Theo. It was the ministry of Van Gogh that was to prove for both Nouwen and his students the most meaningful of all his classes at Yale.

> I still remember how we would spend long hours together in silence, simply gazing at the slides of Vincent's work. I did not try to explain much or analyze much. I simply wanted the students to have a direct experience of the ecstasy and the agony of this painter who shared his desperate search for meaning ... a similar effect resulted from the readings of Vincent's letters. Their haunting, passionate expression of longing for a God who is tangible and alive, who truly comforts and

consoles, and who truly cares for the poor and the suffering brought us in touch with the deepest yearnings of our soul. Vincent's God, so real, so direct, so visible in nature and people, so intensely compassionate, so weak and vulnerable, and so radically loving, was a God we all wanted to come close to.[29]

A student in Nouwen's classes on Van Gogh at Yale Divinity School of 1979, Carol Berry, another émigré (this time from Switzerland), looks back and records that Nouwen had asked Van Gogh's nephew, also named Vincent (1890-1978), why he thought his uncle's paintings so popular. Young Van Gogh responded, 'Because Vincent offers comfort. He was able to crawl under the skin of nature and people and find there something truthful, something beautiful, something joyful. He was able to draw out the inner secret of what he saw.'[30] These words at a timely meeting between Henri Nouwen and Vincent van Gogh the nephew in 1975 (the nephew was to die only three years later, in 1978) prompted the former to begin his studies on Van Gogh the artist.

In a comment that throws much light on the influence Van Gogh had on Nouwen, Berry recounts that Nouwen told his students at Yale:

> I feel close to Vincent because I think that he is a man who really struggled with real spiritual questions and therefore has a lot to say to people who search for God in their lives and want to bring good news to their fellow human beings. The longer I live, the more I try to make sense out of my own struggles, the more I find Vincent to be a real companion. In a strange way I consider him my saint.[31]

Like Nouwen, Van Gogh, of course, was a Dutchman. Both men experienced great emotional trials, including struggling with feelings of shame. Both men's fathers had unmatchable expectations of their sons. Van Gogh came from a religious family, his father was a pastor in the Dutch Reformed church, serving a succession of small Protestant parishes in the predominantly Roman Catholic South of the Netherlands. Van Gogh himself was to leave behind the Groningen 'school' of theology with its Arminian doctrines that he grew up with and join the evangelical wing. Both Van Gogh and Nouwen responded to a vocation to religious service early in their lives. Van Gogh attended theological school in Brussels (although he was refused admission to the seminary in Amsterdam). Both flourished after leaving their native countries, Van Gogh to England and France, Nouwen to America, finding places where each was more comfortable and where life could be lived to the fullest possible extent, where solidarity could be found with the people to whom they ministered.

Van Gogh's early ecclesiastical ministry is little known and it is pertinent for reference to be made to it here, not least for the light it throws on Van Gogh's own experiences and outlook, and, not least, his growth in compassion. In early 1873, after almost four years of working in The Hague for Goupils, a leading international firm of art dealers, Van Gogh was promoted and came to work for Goupils in London. After leaving the firm at the start of April 1876, during which time he had twice visited Paris, Van Gogh applied for teaching positions in Southern England. While in England, Van Gogh 'had long made a habit of attending the services of a variety of Christian denominations; he had no time for doctrinal disputes, believing the differences between the churches were unimportant.'[32] Soon, moving to South London, in addition to teaching in what can only loosely be described as church schools, he attended first Congregational and then Methodist services, becoming a valued helper, an earnest Sunday School teacher, an ardent leader of children's services, speaker, and, at last and with much joy, a Local Lay Preacher:

> When I was standing in the pulpit, I felt like somebody who, emerging from a dark cave underground, comes back to the friendly daylight. It is a delightful thought that in the future, wherever I go, I shall preach the gospel.[33]

It was a joy that was to be all too shortly lived. Unable to be funded for university because of his parents' want of money, Van Gogh went in 1878 on a mission as a lay preacher to the poor working in the poverty-stricken mines in the Borinage, in the south of Belgium under the auspices of the Belgian Missionary Society. Nouwen joined a similar work placement programme in the mines of South Limburg, and later gained experience at Unilever in Rotterdam. The Borinage was a major evangelical target area. In the village of Pâturages, Van Gogh worked independently for several weeks in December 1878. The following year Van Gogh worked, this time for six months, at Wasmes, another village in the Borinage. The people and the living conditions stirred Van Gogh to pity and compassion. As we read in *Compassion*, 'the call to community as we hear it from our Lord is the call to move away from the ordinary and proper places.'[34] Van Gogh's physical displacement inevitably led to a displacement in his painting as we shall see later in this chapter. Van Gogh entered fully into this displacement, as did Nouwen when he moved to live in L'Arche.

However, in July 1879, the Wasmes Chapter, or Consistory, of the Union of Protestant Churches of Belgium rather curiously dispensed with Van Gogh's services. Were the authorities embarrassed by his living the life of the miners too fully? Alarmed by his lack of attention to physical appearance? Ashamed by his awkward style of preaching? There is no clear or straightforward answer. In spite of this, Van Gogh remained in the Borinage for more than a year, living in great poverty in the village of Cuesmes and working independently as an evangelist. Van Gogh's disappointment was bitter:

> I must tell you that with evangelists it is the same as with artists. There is an old academic school, often detestable, tyrannical, the accumulation of horrors, men who wear a cuirass, a steel armour, of prejudices and conventions; when these people are in charge of affairs, they dispose of positions, and by a system of red tape they try to keep their protégés in their places and to exclude the other man.[35]

In the autumn of 1880, Van Gogh, still bitter against the 'evangelical gentlemen' whom he compared with the 'academic' artists of the day as 'physically, emotionally, and spiritually spent,'[36] made the crucial decision to become an artist and applied himself wholeheartedly to painting.

Although Van Gogh left the Church in 1880 because of his frustration with his perceived hypocrisy of the clergy, particularly that of his father and uncle, he continued to hold to many aspects of his former faith: his respect for the Bible, his love of and for the person of Jesus, his concern for the poor and his belief in a revolution that would bring about the kingdom of God on earth, as well as the reward of an afterlife for those who had suffered the earthly journey of faith. This last was possibly informed by Van Gogh's formation with the Methodists for whom universalism was, and continues to be, a basic tenet of faith. Ever faithful, 'Van Gogh's religious feelings were always linked with his compassion for the poor and outcast.'[37] It was this link that was to compel Van Gogh to retrieve an authentically Christian vision of the world and to have such a profound impact on Nouwen.

In a very real sense, Van Gogh's ministry continued, now through a transfigured and transfiguring medium, that of painting, and his notions of the central and basic importance of religion pervade his artistic work. Although many have argued that Van Gogh left his former faith, it is more accurate to say he left the institutional Church but not Christianity itself, seeking an integration of his faith with modernity. There is a revealing comment of Nouwen, regarding the church as an institution, in a letter written to John Garvey, a long-standing friend, which is relevant here. Nouwen writes, 'I am planning to take a year off next year [1970-71] ... I will probably rent a small apartment in Utrecht and join the less churchy people. *I think that many important religious things are happening outside the walls of our church* and I would like to experience it.'[38] At no point did Van Gogh denigrate the Bible but deeply believed modern literature supplemented the scriptures. He experienced the divine in the most mundane acts. His representing the infinite in the finite was to be one of the prevailing signatures of his expression.

Both Van Gogh and Nouwen, constantly fearing rejection and solitude, especially from those they loved, sank into periods of deep depression, yet, at their lowest ebb, created some of their most inspiring and memorable work, driven by the pain they were experiencing. It was to Van Gogh that Nouwen was to turn to reclaim times of 'personal restoration and renewal.'[39]

Van Gogh generally avoided painting biblical scenes and traditional religious subjects, arguing that these would be based on his imagination. How, then, did he inspire the religious in Nouwen? By observing God's world. His portraits and landscapes brought to life a vision of the world that is transfused with God's presence and transformed into a new reality. Gone, for the most part, are representations of angels, martyrs, and saints. Present are images of foreheads and cheeks blocked out in a vivid green or red, vibrant sunflowers and cypresses stage-managed on glorious canvases, and evocative cloud formations.

It may well be argued that Nouwen was mentored by Van Gogh through his paintings. It may also be argued that Van Gogh, whose life sounded so many resonances with Nouwen's own, touched Nouwen more deeply than Thomas Merton. Despite living before him, Van Gogh (as was the case, of course, with Rembrandt) touched Nouwen's heart, too, through his art, through his creativity. Nouwen came to know the creator and the Creator. All of which fascinated Nouwen. Shortly before his death, Nouwen wrote:

> All the people he paints are radiant like saints and his orchids, cypresses and wheat fields are burning with the fire of his intense feelings.[40]

> Through his oils and pastels he was able to unite the visible world with the world of his heart.[41]

While teaching at Yale Divinity School, as Associate and then Full Professor in Pastoral Theology (1971-81), Nouwen offered seminars titled 'The Compassion of Vincent van Gogh', and 'The Ministry of Vincent van Gogh', which both he and his students considered the deepest, most effective classes of his career there, having made a more profound impression on his students than any of his other courses. Indeed, in a conversation with Edwards, Nouwen confessed that he never found students 'more personally, intellectually, and emotionally involved than during those periods of attentive looking at Vincent's drawings and paintings.'[42]

Manifestly, the heart of Van Gogh's art is his gift to express the compassion of God, recognised by Nouwen and his fellow students through silence. As

Edwards himself noted, he, too, saw Vincent van Gogh as, 'an artist who out of compassion sacrificed himself to fashion a new art of the spirit that would speak to ordinary people, bringing comfort and healing.'[43]

'This deeply wounded and immensely gifted Dutchman brought me in touch with my own brokenness and talents in ways nobody else could'

Nouwen found in Van Gogh a similar focus and meditative spirit as his own. 'Few writers or painters have influenced me as much as Vincent', he recorded. 'This deeply wounded and immensely gifted Dutchman brought me in touch with my own brokenness and talents in ways nobody else could.'[44] Here was a man with a sincere yearning and a true insight into the presence of God in the world. From Van Gogh's paintings and letters Nouwen became aware of God in every conceivable place and situation. For Van Gogh's part, in a letter to his brother, Theo, Vincent writes 'To me to believe in God is to feel that there is a God, not dead or stuffed, but alive, urging us toward *aimer encore* (steadfast love) with irresistible force' (23 November 1881). It throws much light on the church authorities of the time when one reads that Van Gogh, in a desire to help others, pursued a calling as a minister but was refused admission to the seminary in Amsterdam, and, again, when adopting a lifestyle similar to that of the coal miners in southern Belgium to whom he ministered and by whom he was quickly befriended, he was soon removed by the church authorities.

Although Van Gogh severed all ties with institutional religion, he did not lose his passion for God's mystery, and, in a way, this freed him up to see God in other ways. Thus, we perceive the symbolism in *Starry Night*, *La Berceuse*, *The Potato Eaters*, and *At Eternity's Gate* as it expresses in such paintings the close tie between the painter and God. Van Gogh, spurned by the church authorities, never felt spurned by God, and his 'deep reverence for God in nature and his deep compassion for struggling and marginal members of society suggest why Nouwen held both Van Gogh and his artistry in such high regard.'[45] Van Gogh, in breaking through the ecclesiastical barriers, came and remained close to God. In remaining close to God, he was able to let go of status and start his downwardly mobile life. Certainly, it was a life full of difficulties, a life full of challenges, but in these difficulties and challenges, Van Gogh was enabled to enter into the lives of others and become a channel of God's compassion, both for himself and for them. There is a sentence in *Compassion* which sums this up well:

> Voluntary displacement leads us to the existential recognition of our inner brokenness and thus brings us to a deeper solidarity with the brokenness of our fellow human beings.[46]

Such a displacement was eminently manifest in Van Gogh's life.

While Nouwen was at Yale, he spent two sabbaticals at the Trappist Abbey of the Genesee, in Piffard, upstate New York, the first from June to December 1974, when he kept the first of five journals, *The Genesee Diary*,[47] the second from February to July 1979, when *A Cry for Mercy*, a series of contextualised prayers from his prayer journal, was written.[48] The first sabbatical in particular was a formative time for him[49] and his popularity as a writer increased after the publication of *The Genesee Diary*.[50] Another product of the first sabbatical was *Reaching Out*,[51] the material of which had already been taught in a Christian spirituality seminar at Yale but was edited and refined during these months and published three years later. In the book Nouwen records his intention to articulate his 'most personal thoughts and feelings about being a Christian.'[52] It was his first attempt to set down a concise description of Christian spirituality and, full of references to Catholic and non-Catholic ministers, religious, and theologians, has been described as a 'pivotal work in his output'.[53] Moreover, it is his first work in which he describes the spiritual life as encompassing three relationships – relationship to God, to self, and to others – that were to prove foundational in his approach to compassion.[54] Nouwen was to return to the abbey for many other visits, and he used it as a base for fifteen months from July 1981, that is after his resignation from Yale, whilst he fulfilled various speaking and writing engagements.[55]

This was the natural continuation of the *mysterium passionis* about which Nouwen spoke to John Garvey, a priest in the Antiochian Orthodox Church and a long-time friend of Nouwen, in the early 1980s: 'compassion in the most profound sense, is suffering with God; it is an entering into the passion of God.'[56] It is a development of all that Nouwen had discovered in Van Gogh and it is a spiritual insight that people from all traditions within the Christian faith can relate to and benefit from.

'One must paint the peasants as being one of them, *as feeling, thinking as they do*'

Van Gogh had a focus and meditative spirit similar to Nouwen's, a sincere and deep yearning for a 'comforting and consoling God',[57] and true insight into God's presence in the world. From his subjects, the glance of an old seaman, the tilted bonnet of a faded beauty, the alleyways, the fields, emanated a Zen-like awareness of the presence of God. Indeed, Van Gogh owed as much to Japanese models as to European ones, once again making a profound impact on Nouwen. Nouwen told Edwards of 'receiving courage for his own search through his experience of Vincent's search,'[58] describing Van Gogh as 'one of the main spiritual guides of my life':[59]

Although Vincent van Gogh is certainly not a religious writer in the traditional sense of the word, for me he was a man whose spirit touched my spirit very deeply, and who brought me in touch with some aspects of the spiritual life that no formal spiritual writer ever did.[60]

With Van Gogh's influence, Nouwen's understanding of compassion had made that all important journey from the head to the heart. Thereby, coming eight years after Nouwen's meeting with Merton, Nouwen's opening up to the life and work of Van Gogh marked a decisive move forward in the former's understanding of the Christian life in general, and of the central part compassion has to play in particular.

It was through painting that Van Gogh was able to connect to that great Source of creative energy and see in creation the symbols of a loving and consoling Divine Presence.

> I think that everything which is really good and beautiful – of inner moral, spiritual and sublime beauty in men and their works – comes from God, and that which is bad and wrong in men and in their works is not of God, and God does not approve of it. But I think that the best way to know God is to love many things.[61]

In his *At Eternity's Gate* (*Old Man in Sorrow*), there is a sentiment that is 'far from all theology'. Anti-clerical, anti-institutional though he was, Van Gogh remained deeply religious *and deeply spiritual*. At the very depths of his pain and sorrow, he was able to rest in God and eternity, writing about this painting that 'there is something noble, something great, which cannot be destined for the worms ... this is far from all theology, simply the fact that the poorest little woodcutter or peasant on the hearth or miner can have moments of emotion and inspiration that give him a feeling of an eternal home, and of being close to it.'[62]

> We are pilgrims on the earth and strangers – we have come from afar and we are going far – the journey of our life goes from the loving breast of our Mother on earth to the arms of our Father in heaven. Everything on earth changes – we have no abiding city here – it is the experience of everybody. That it is God's will that we should part with what is dearest on earth – we ourselves change in many respects, we are not what we once were, we shall not remain what we are now.[63]

Van Gogh's sermon, from which these lines are taken, were to have an obvious influence on Nouwen (spilling over into the influence that the paintings of Rembrandt were also to have on him). *Making All Things New, In the House of the Lord*, and *The Inner Voice of Love* all bear this out. Also remarkable are the words written by Van Gogh in the autumn of 1880 when he decided to turn to painting and, in this way, rest in God. Writing in a style that is akin to the Prodigal when he 'comes to himself,' Van Gogh reflects:

> It was when I was in just such deep misery that I felt my energies revive, and I said to myself: In spite of everything I shall rise again; I will take up my pencil, which I have forsaken in my great discouragement, and I will go on with my drawing. And from that moment everything has seemed transformed for me; and now I have started, and my pencil has become a little more docile with every day.[64]

It was Van Gogh's ability to rise, like the Prodigal, from the very depths of despair in which he had known others and to find rest in God that enabled Nouwen, also, to love all others, especially, perhaps, those on the margins of society, in Central and South America, on the Civil Rights Marches, and, ultimately, of course, at L'Arche.

Van Gogh's depiction of Nature, above all his indisputably visionary *Starry Night*, of June 1889, which was possibly inspired by – but, arguably, outranks – the painting of the same title by Millet (1814-75), is, I believe, a sublime depiction of *kenosis*. Under the huge moon and radiant, quivering sun or stars, the cypress and landscape tremble, moving in empathy with each other. Alone, the little village remains stolidly empty and still in the 'turbulent vastness of the universe.'[65] And it was, moreover, through such paintings that Van Gogh was able to portray the connection between God and His creation, a connection made manifest in Jesus that was to prove fundamental in Nouwen's own life and ministry.

> Vincent felt profoundly that, through nature, the presence of God was revealed. This sensuous and earthy longing to find God in all that surrounded him was what Henri affirmed. It was a longing for a God who would not abandon humanity but rather permeate all creation with the divine presence. It was a God who lived among poor peasants, miners, the lonely and oppressed, and who comforted them and shone his love and light into the darkest corners of their lives.[66]

For example, Van Gogh's masterpiece *The Potato Eaters* depicts a family crowded together sharing a simple meal. Van Gogh wrote that he painted the figures in the dark colours of a 'very dusty, unpeeled potato'[67] The painting's one unifying element is the lamp with its warm glow piercing the pervading atmosphere of isolation. Its yellow light is Van Gogh's symbol of love, recalling the gospel, the central presence of Jesus.

There is a beautiful sentence in *Compassion* which comes to mind here:

> When we are led by love instead of driven by fear, we can enter the places of the greatest darkness and pain and experience in a unique way the power of God's care.[68]

Van Gogh was enabled to experience this and Nouwen was increasingly able to do this, as his love for others grew stronger.

Painting was always a means for Van Gogh and never an end in itself. About his painting, Van Gogh wrote, 'One must paint the peasants as being one of them, as feeling, thinking as they do.'[69] This is compassion in, perhaps, its most humble and sincere form. In this humility Van Gogh, in his own eyes, became a nonentity, or an eccentric and disagreeable man – somebody who has no position in society and never will have, in short, the lowest of the low.[70] In his downward mobility, Van Gogh came closer to the meek, the poor, and the despised – in a word 'the poor in spirit' of the beatitudes[71] (a concept Vanier was to develop through his work with L'Arche) – and found God there. It was more than simply some kind of Christ-like downward mobility, for this might, at some point, involve some feeling of upward mobility, too. It was, rather, a kind of downward growth, a growth that implies pain, risk and struggle, a growth that Nouwen experienced on leaving academia for L'Arche. The paradox of voluntary displacement is unpacked in *Compassion*:

> Although it seems to separate us from the world – from father, mother, brothers, sisters, family, and friends – we actually find ourselves in deeper union with it. Voluntary displacement leads to compassionate living precisely because it moves us from positions of distinction to positions of sameness, from being in special places to being everywhere.[72]

Let me take just one other example of Van Gogh's downward growth. When Van Gogh decided to leave the hospitable home of a miner's family to go and live in the hovel of a very needy family, he wrote to the miner's wife, 'Esther, one should do like the good God; from time to time one should go and live among his own.'[73] Very much an example of Nouwen's downward mobility before its time. Like Merton, Van Gogh (later Vanier, and – as far as he could – Nouwen) cleared his mind and spirit of attachments and temptations through prayer, simplicity and solitude, cultivating humility, love and compassion and developing an awareness of his own *real* self, with Christ at the centre, liberating himself in order to recognise Christ in the other person. This recalls some sentences in *Compassion* on the purposes of God's own displacement:

God became displaced so that nothing human would be alien and the brokenness of our human condition could be fully experienced.[74]

And again:

Jesus' call to voluntary displacement has a very contemporary ring. It is obviously not a call to disruptive behavior, but a call to solidarity with the millions who live disrupted lives.[75]

Van Gogh, himself, discovered in Victor Hugo (1802-85) a man of like mind. Here was an author who combined a belief in the virtue of the poor and downtrodden with an awakening to the romance of living more fully. In *Les Misérables*, Hugo writes, 'To love another person is to see the face of God.' In his *Still Life with Open Bible and Zola Novel*, Van Gogh depicts his father's large Bible propped open at Isaiah 53, the Old Testament passage on the Suffering Servant.[76] Here was the heart of scripture: an afflicted and cast-off figure, suffering in misery and yet bearing God's promise. The mystery of God revealed through the meek and the poor, even the despised. Could this be Van Gogh's depiction of himself as 'despised and rejected,' by the church authorities, 'a man of sorrows, and acquainted with grief' amongst the miners and their families in the Borinage?

Also depicted in *Still Life* is the novel, *La Joie de Vivre* (1884), by Émile Zola (1840-1902) a much smaller book yet more dominant on account of its colour, utterly modern and, on account of the brutal naturalism of his descriptions, controversial. Zola's books 'were among Van Gogh's great enthusiasms, almost incomprehensible to the Pastor and conventionally pious people of his generation ... The passage from Isaiah speaks of suffering and promises redemption; in *La Joie de Vivre* the redemption is ever-present in the unconquerable vitality and love of life that carries the principal character through all her misfortunes,'[77] the Suffering Servant in modern dress, a theme that resounds like a motif throughout much of Nouwen's writing, especially on ministry.[78]

As they begin the first chapter of *Compassion*, the three writers remind the reader of the prophet Isaiah's words recalled in Mt 1:22-23, "'The Virgin shall conceive and give birth to a son and they will call him 'Immanuel,' a name which means 'God-is-with-us'". In order for the reader to be able to feel and know something more of this 'divine solidarity', they explore 'the experience of [feeling and knowing] someone being truly with us.'[79] They write that 'we have lost the simple but difficult gift of being present to each other,'[80] and the reason for this loss is that 'we have been led to believe that presence must be *useful*.'[81] We shy away from showing compassion because we think we cannot do or say anything that might be 'useful'. We have forgotten that in being 'useless', that is to say in simply being present, we can, in fact, bring comfort and consolation because, putting control and self-determination aside, we can enter into the other's powerlessness and weakness. We can share in the other's vulnerability. Those who offer us comfort and consolation by being and staying with us in times of anguish, darkness, or illness show their solidarity with us by 'willingly entering the dark, uncharted spaces of our lives. For this reason, they are the ones who bring new hope and help us discover new directions.'[82]

This 'divine solidarity does not mean that God solves our problems, shows us the way out of our confusion, or offers answers for our many questions.'[83] No, he does far more than that. 'The solidarity of God consists in the fact that God is willing to enter with us into our problems, confusions, and questions.'[84] To do the former would disable, rather than enable. God 'is moved by our pains and participates in the fullness of the human struggle.'[85]

In an article published in March 1976, Nouwen describes three gifts of the Holy Spirit (he calls them 'three aspects of compassion') that were present in Van Gogh's life: solidarity, consolation, and comfort. Having considered the two aspects of solidarity and consolation, let's move forward to reflect on the importance of the aspect of comfort.

'A new way of seeing, a new way of living'

Van Gogh's life was a quest for unification, a seeking to integrate religion, art, literature, and nature. Experience led him to deepen and simplify his understanding of the unifying power of love. Van Gogh, experiencing a deep solidarity with miners, for instance, writes in a letter to Theo, 'Let us ask that our part in life should be to become the poor in the kingdom of God, God's servants.[86] When we see the images of the indescribable and unutterable desolation, of loneliness, of poverty and misery, the end of all things, or their extreme, then there arises in our mind the thought of God ... I want to do drawings which touch some people ... I want to progress so far that people will say of my work: he feels deeply, he feels tenderly.'[87] 'That', responds Nouwen, 'was his vocation: to touch people by tenderly expressing his solidarity with the human condition—not by anger but by love.'[88]

In paintings such as *Head of Woman with her hair loose*, *Peasant Woman, Digging*, and *Exercise Yard at Newgate Gaol* Van Gogh touched the deep and frequently hidden human sorrow that unites each one of us, and brought it to the surface in order for it to be noticed and to console, to show solidarity *cum solo*, with the lonely other. Nouwen reflects, 'Consolation indeed asks for the sincere struggle to reach into the center of human brokenness; out of its common depths compassion can be expressed.'[89]

For Nouwen, 'one of Vincent van Gogh's most remarkable talents was his ability to offer comfort,'[90] and this was the reason his nephew offered for the fascination expressed in the second half of the twentieth century with his uncle's paintings. Van Gogh's depictions of the sun, casting its light over the wheat fields of Arles, rising behind the sower, replacing Jesus in his painting of the resurrection of Lazarus, are famous. 'Those who see Vincent's sun feel the warmth of his comfort and understand that his solidarity and consolation make them see the rays of the great sun in their deepest selves. They realize that he was a compassionate man.'[91]

The voluntary displacement which Van Gogh experienced during his own life enabled him to come alongside others and offer comfort. Van Gogh's situation is summed up extremely well in *Compassion*, at the end of the chapter on displacement:

> Voluntary displacement is part of the life of each Christian. It leads away from the ordinary and proper places ... it leads to a recognition of each other as fellow travellers on the road, and thus creates community ... voluntary displacement leads to compassion; by bringing us closer to our own brokenness it opens our eyes to our fellow human beings, who seek our consolation and comfort.[92]

As I have already argued, it is in Van Gogh's representations of the everyday working person that compassion is seen,[93] evidencing a downward mobility, similar to Nouwen's own.[94] Disillusioned with organised religion,[95] there remains a reverence for God and an abiding compassion for struggling and marginal members of society made manifest in the portraits of Roulin, the mailman in Arles, the portraits of Roulin's wife (in particular *La Berceuse*), and the man depicted in *Prayer Before the Meal* and paintings such as the ground-breaking *The Potato Eaters* (1885), and *At Eternity's Gate* (1890). About the former, Van Gogh wrote, 'I have tried to emphasize that these people, eating their potatoes in the lamplight, have dug the earth with those very hands they put into the dish, and so it speaks of manual labour and the way in which they have earned their food.'[96] As Erickson has written:

> The expression of the infinite in the mundane, Van Gogh's experience of the numinous quality of day to day human existence, pervades his work. Rather than choosing the subject matter and the iconography of traditional religious painting to express the divine presence, Van Gogh instead tried to capture what he saw of the infinite in the commonplace subjects of everyday life.[97]

In the nineteenth century, the most acceptable and desirable subjects for painting were biblical or mythological, followed by landscape, and still life. Paintings of peasants at that time dressed and clean as china dolls, were regarded as the most base. Van Gogh's realistic portrayal of labourers, miners and peasants was regarded as being in the worst possible taste. Van Gogh explained:

> I prefer painting people's eyes to cathedrals, for there is something in the eyes that is not in the cathedral, however solemn and imposing the latter may be – a human soul, be it that of a poor beggar or of a street walker, is more interesting to me.[98]

His depictions of peasants reflect his own admiration for Christian humility. He imbued even prostitutes with a sacred quality and captured this reverence for the piety of the meek, poor, and simple in his first major work of his Dutch period, *The Potato Eaters*. As he wrote to Wilhelmina van Gogh, Van Gogh's youngest sister, 'To be perfumed is not what a peasant picture needs.'[99]

Leaving the coal mines and going to France, Van Gogh dedicated his life to expressing through his art his deeply felt conviction that God was present in all that surrounded him. He wanted others to perceive this too.

> Compassion manifests itself first of all in the consciousness of being part of humanity, in the awareness of the oneness of the human race, in the intimate knowledge that all people, wherever they dwell in time or place, are bound together by the same human condition. Through this inner sense of solidarity and consolation, the even deeper bond with all of creation can be sensed – and that gives us strength.[100]
>
> When one lives with others and is united by a feeling of affection, one is aware of a reason for living and perceives that one is not quite worthless and superfluous, but perhaps good for something; we need each other and make the same journey as travelling companions.[101]

Carol Berry comments that 'Vincent van Gogh, while training to be a lay missionary, had realized over a hundred years before Nouwen was lecturing on compassion at Yale that his oppressed parishioners did not need theologically sound sermons but basic compassionate understanding along with practical support for managing the struggles of daily life.'[102]

It is not difficult to be aware of the tremendous debt Nouwen paid to Van Gogh. In the closing lines of his Foreword to Cliff Edwards' book, *Van Gogh and God*, Nouwen writes that he now realises why Van Gogh had such a deep effect on him. 'Cliff Edwards' study', Nouwen writes, 'makes it clear that Vincent wants not only to lead us to a new way of seeing but also to a new way of living.' It seems to me that Nouwen, too, by his life and writing, can lead us not only to a new way of seeing the Church in all its multi-faceted work but also to a new way of living out our vocation as Christians. Van Gogh, Nouwen continues, 'invites us through his art to a change of heart.' For Nouwen, Van Gogh was always 'a minister' and it is for this reason, he concludes, 'we experience a call to conversion.' This, Nouwen writes, 'is the deepest reason for [Van Gogh's] universal appeal.'[103]

The way of Van Gogh, of course, was the way of Christ. In *In the House of the Lord* there is a passage in a chapter headed 'Fecundity and Love' that describes the way of God. 'The way of God', Nouwen begins, 'is the way of weakness. The great news of the Gospel is precisely that God became small and vulnerable, and hence bore fruit among us.' Nouwen continues, 'The most fruitful life ever lived is the life of Jesus, who did not cling to his divine power but became as we are (see Phil 2:6-7). Jesus brought us new life in ultimate vulnerability. He came to us as a small child, dependent on the care and protection of others. He lived for us as a poor preacher, without any political, economic, or military power. He died for us nailed on a cross as a useless criminal. It is in this extreme vulnerability that our salvation was won. The fruit of this poor and failing existence is eternal life for all who believe in him.' Nouwen reflects how humanity might be aware of this vulnerability:

> It is very hard for us to grasp even a little bit of the mystery of God's vulnerability, yet, when we have eyes to see and ears to hear we can see it in so many ways and in many places. We can see it when a child is born, the fruit of the love of two people who came together without defences and embraced each other in weakness. We can see it in the graceful smiles of poor people and in the warm affection of the handicapped. We can see it every time people ask forgiveness and are reconciled.[104]

There is a passage from *Bread for the Journey* (24 May), written during the autumn of 1995, a year before Nouwen died, that describes the poverty of Jesus, which serves as a meditation on the Christological hymn that runs throughout the book *Compassion*:

> Jesus, the Blessed One, is poor. The poverty of Jesus is much more than an economic or social poverty. Jesus is poor because he freely chose powerlessness over power, vulnerability over defensiveness, dependency over self-sufficiency. As the great 'Song of Christ' so beautifully expresses: 'He ... did not count equality with God something to be grasped. But he emptied himself ... becoming as humans are' (Phil 2:6-7). This is the poverty of spirit that Jesus chose to live.[105]

Jesus calls everyone to live their lives with that same poverty. If we receive the humility of God into our hearts, we become able to accept and embrace and love the very poverty which is God, and the stranger at our table, the image of God – again a development of Van Gogh's influence on Nouwen, and a basic spiritual truth that all Christians may share – with fruitful consequences.

In the opening pages of *Compassion*, Nouwen and his co-authors write, 'When we begin to see God, the source of all our comfort and consolation, in the center of servanthood, compassion becomes much more than doing good for unfortunate people.'[106] It is no less than living a new way of life. Not one in which pain and suffering are sought but one in which the God of compassion, through servanthood, is witnessed. Not one in which one simply desires to bring about individual or social change, but one that expresses the common search for God. 'Radical servanthood challenges us ... to reveal the gentle presence of our compassionate God in the midst of our broken world.'[107] 'Compassion' Nouwen insists in *Here and Now*, 'is something other than pity. Pity suggests distance, even a certain condescendence.'[108]

'God's compassion is a compassion that reveals itself in servanthood.'[109] The fullness of God's compassion, McNeill, Morrison, and Nouwen argue, can be seen in Christ. Jesus Christ, God-with-Us, 'has come to us in the freedom of love, not needing to experience our human condition but freely choosing to do so out of love.'[110] With the realisation of this comes the awareness of Christ as Servant, a challenging concept since we do not expect to be liberated, or strengthened, or healed, or led by someone who 'emptied himself.'

Subject to the same powers and influences that dominate everyone, the same anxieties, fears, and uncertainties that we all suffer, Jesus 'did not cling to his equality with God,' but emptied himself, and 'became as we are,' a condition of total dependency.[111] The authors point out that Paul's hymn 'does not ask us to look upward, away from our condition, but to look in our midst *and discover God there*.'[112]

Jesus became fully human 'in the most dejected and rejected way', and experienced 'the most despicable, and horrifying form of death – death on a cross' – experiencing 'the agony, pain, and total degradation of the bloody torture and death of a convicted criminal' and suffering death 'in one of its rawest, ugliest, and most degrading forms.'[113]

This is the price God is willing to pay for intimacy. It is the price of ultimate servanthood, the price of becoming a slave, completely dependent on strange, cruel, alien forces.[114] It is to this compassion-in-action that I turn in the next chapter.

Children carried vases of sunflowers and irises, transforming the barren Communion table into a garden of delight bursting out in yellows, greens, and browns. The flowers, evocative of his father's own gardens, anchored the table in the rich soil of the Netherlands, home also to Van Gogh, whose work Nouwen had loved so deeply.[115]

Chapter 3

Jean Vanier and the invitation to come and discover the treasure of the poor

The full impact of Jean Vanier (1928-) and L'Arche on Henri Nouwen was only experienced after a longer period of gestation. Nouwen's contact with Vanier began in the late 1970s (when Nouwen was a fully-fledged Professor in the faculty of Yale Divinity School) with a strange greeting, which throws some light on Nouwen's lack of domesticity and, I think, lack of a sense of being earthed.

One afternoon a young woman named Jan Risse, who had founded the L'Arche community in Mobile, Alabama, and was one of the federation's co-ordinators in North America, rang the doorbell and entered Nouwen's New Haven apartment. Explaining he had a busy schedule of appointments that day, Nouwen left Jan there for a number of hours. When Nouwen returned that evening, Jan had prepared a lovely evening meal and laid his table with 'a beautiful linen cloth, nice plates and silverware, flowers, a burning candle, and a bottle of wine.'[1] When Nouwen asked, 'What is this?' Jan laughed. 'Oh, I thought I'd make you a nice meal.' 'But where did you find all these things?' 'In your own kitchen and cupboards ... you obviously don't use them too often!'[2] A stranger had walked into Nouwen's home and, without asking him for anything, had, in fact, showed him his own house. Jan remained in town several days and did many acts of kindness and service for Nouwen. When she finally left, she simply said, 'Just remember, Jean Vanier sends his greetings to you.'[3]

At the time the visit seemed 'uneventful' and even 'inconsequential'[4] but after a few years, in 1981, when he had forgotten all about the visit, Nouwen received a telephone call out of the blue one morning from Vanier inviting him to join him on a short, silent, Pentecost covenant retreat with some of the L'Arche assistants in South Bend, near Chicago. For a moment Nouwen again thought that Vanier wanted him to give a talk but the latter insisted, 'This is a *silent* retreat. We can just be together and pray.'[5]

As the years passed by, Nouwen and Vanier had a number of long discussions. Nouwen also invited Vanier to Harvard and Vanier writes, 'He was an incredible teacher. I sensed just how much the students loved him.'[6]

These intervening years were full of anxiety and tumult, with Jean Vanier's voice heard only at times in the background. After ten years at Yale, Nouwen felt 'a deep desire to return to a more basic ministry'[7] and considered spending the rest of his life among the poor of Bolivia or Peru. In 1981 he resigned from his teaching position at Yale and journeyed to Bolivia but soon discovered that his true vocation did not lie here. He returned to North America and, for a time, taught at Harvard Divinity School. However, Nouwen felt that this was not where God wanted him to be, either.

Two years later, Nouwen's lecturing at Harvard Divinity School was combined with further time spent in Central and South America, and also in France, at the L'Arche community at Trosly-Breuil. His reputation as a writer continued to rocket, his readership now including a substantial inter-faith element.

As soon as Harvard's Spring semester of 1983 was over, Nouwen visited Mexico and Nicaragua, then Peru.[8] On returning to the United States in September, he embarked upon a two-month lecture tour, directing his audiences to tell their president, Ronald Reagan (1911 – 2004; President 1981–1989), to stay out of Central American politics.[9]

It was during the autumn of 1983 that Jean Vanier, the founder of L'Arche, invited a by now exhausted Nouwen to visit him at L'Arche in Trosly-Breuil.[10] Nouwen was to stay in France for six weeks. Nouwen's stay with Vanier, from November to December 1983, at L'Arche in Trosly – during which time he came across a poster reproduction of *The Return of the Prodigal Son* by Rembrandt van Rijn – was to prove a turning point in the former's spiritual journey that was to be realised more fully later.[11] Jean Vanier writes 'Henri Nouwen was a Dutch Catholic priest who had spent much of his life teaching at universities in the United States. After we met, I invited him to come visit us at Trosly, and a few years later he gave up teaching to become the pastor at L'Arche-Daybreak, assuming a role much like that of Père Thomas at Trosly.'[12]

When Nouwen went back to Harvard for the spring semester of 1984, he made the commitment to return to Trosly-Breuil the next Christmas for a thirty-day retreat. During this second visit he started to realise that Jan Risse's early visit was a response to his prayer, 'Lord, show me where you want me to go, and I will follow you.'[13] Nouwen's encounter with Vanier had created a turning point in the former's spiritual journey to be realised in full only later.

After the spring semester in 1984, Nouwen made another trip to Latin America, in particular Guatemala, and, during the following year, published *Love in a Fearful Land: A Guatemalan Story*,[14] before returning to Trosly-Breuil for a Christmas retreat.

Nouwen was unhappy at Harvard. 'It's not an intimate place, not a home,' Nouwen wrote. 'It's a place of intellectual battle.'[15] Vanier, too, noted that Nouwen knew he couldn't stay: 'It might have been a growing loneliness. Or it might have been the discrepancy between who he was and what he was living in an interior and personal sense, and the acclaim he was receiving from the students. My feeling was that somewhere there was a discrepancy between those two elements which became almost unbearable for him.'[16] Although he enjoyed teaching, and his audiences continued to be capacity ones, Nouwen found the environment extremely difficult. He yearned for community but perceived Harvard to be even more competitive than Yale and many of the faculty members pretentious.[17] Robert Jonas, a student at Harvard and a personal friend records:

> Henri's shameless declaration of Christ's living presence among us was probably an embarrassment to some of his Harvard colleagues and students who were used to the fine, dispassionate art of theological reasoning.[18]

Nouwen writes at some length about Vanier's visit to Harvard in his Foreword to the latter's *From Brokenness to Community*. It is a far less vitriolic and more balanced description than those that he gave on leaving Harvard, going so far as to write that he 'loved' teaching there but perhaps this was Nouwen at his most accommodating, bearing in mind that the book for which he was providing the Foreword were of lectures given by Vanier there.

> It was that tall, self-confident, poorly dressed, but aristocratic looking man who had made me wonder whether Harvard was the best place for me. I loved teaching there. I was excited about the great variety of students and felt challenged by the questions they, especially the women students, were raising. But Harvard didn't feel like home for me. Somehow I knew that I was looking for something that could nurture my heart in a more basic way and offer me a better context for my spiritual growth. When I met Jean Vanier for the first time, I immediately sensed that he not only understood the desire of my soul, but also knew how to respond to it. He invited me to come to his community and discover the treasure of the poor. It wasn't immediately clear to me that I should leave Harvard and join L'Arche, but, on knowing Jean, a search was set

in motion that finally led me to leave the academic world and join the life with mentally handicapped people.[19]

Nouwen taught one more semester at Harvard in 1985, visited Haiti, and then resigned from Harvard. In an open letter to his friends, Nouwen penned:

> It was a hard decision to make, but after a long and often painful time of discernment I came to the conclusion that Harvard is not the right place for me. I felt unable to maintain the vitality of spirit necessary to teach about the spiritual life.[20]

Later he was to confess:

> After twenty-five years of priesthood, I found myself praying poorly, living somewhat isolated from other people, and very much preoccupied with burning issues ... I woke up one day with the realization that I was living in a very dark place and that the term 'burnout' was a convenient psychological translation for a spiritual death.[21]

In August 1985 Nouwen left academia for life with people with and without living disabilities in L'Arche, first, in order to discern his way forward, in Trosly-Breuil, France, and then, off and on for the remainder of his life, at Daybreak. On reading that there was a home for him in L'Arche, a place where he would be loved and called to grow,[22] and listening to Vanier in Trosly-Breuil, Nouwen was to realise he was being called to live with a different type of so-called 'poor'.[23] During his months at L'Arche Nouwen completed two more books: *Lifesigns*,[24] known in the United Kingdom by its English title *In the House of the Lord: The Journey from Fear to Love*, focusing on John 15 and abiding in the love of Jesus, and *Behold the Beauty of the Lord*,[25] a series of meditations on icons, and one of the best introductions to the subject. Interestingly, although *Lifesigns/In the House of the Lord* is based upon lectures given by Nouwen at Harvard, the university itself is never mentioned in Nouwen's text. It is, instead, dedicated to Madame Pauline Vanier, Jean Vanier's mother.

Touched by God's spirit

We arrive now at one of the most significant turning points in Nouwen's life. Nouwen said that his life had been dominated by two voices, his father's – urging him to be 'independent, self-sufficient and competent and have something to show the world' – and his mother's – inviting him to 'love Jesus above all else.' After resigning from Harvard, Nouwen was invited by Vanier to once again return to Trosly-Breuil, this time to stay for a year in part of his mother's house. The invitation was to prove pivotal. In *Letter 7 to Marc*, entitled 'On listening to Jesus', Nouwen writes from Trosly:

> In mid-August I went to Canada to live and work at 'Daybreak', the L'Arche community near Toronto ... My year in Europe was meant to be a period of searching for a new direction in my life. I had a vague notion that Jesus was calling me to leave the university and to go and live with mentally handicapped people. My meeting with Jean Vanier and my stay in the L'Arche community at Trosly awoke in me something new which I couldn't continue to ignore. The burning question was: 'How best am I to follow Jesus?'[26]

Nouwen was in Trosly from August 1985 until July 1986. At Christmas time he gave 'Mammie' Vanier a photograph of an icon of *The Bridegroom*, depicting John the Evangelist leaning against Jesus' breast, which Robert Lentz (1946-) had made for him. Pauline Vanier expressed her gratitude by telling him about her deep devotion to the heart of Jesus. She also told him about Père Almire Pichon SJ (1843-1919) who had been the spiritual director of Thérèse of Lisieux (1873-97) and Pauline's own mother. It was from Pichon and her own mother that Pauline had acquired her deep devotion to the Sacred Heart.

In his meditation on John 19:31-37, the heart of Jesus becomes, for Nouwen, 'the sacred place where all that was, is, and ever shall be is held in unity.'[27] The blood of Jesus, 'flows from your broken heart to heal my broken heart and the broken hearts of every man and woman in every time and place.'[28] The water flowing from the broken heart of Jesus, 'makes me into a new person, a child of your Father, and your brother. It is the water of baptism that has been poured over me and so many others and that has given entrance to the new community fashioned by your Spirit.'[29]

Pauline Vanier and Nouwen became close friends. Nouwen believed his invitation was a gift from God in order to enable him to discern His divine will. One commentator, Mary Uhler, remarked that Jean Vanier became the 'voice' of Nouwen's mother.[30] Together, Vanier and L'Arche called Nouwen back to a life of prayer and the nurturing of his relationship with Jesus. They enabled this 'homeless' man to keep in touch with his heart through solitude and prayer and enlarge his heart through loving those with whom he came into daily contact. For twelve months he ate, played, worked, and prayed with – and learnt from – people with learning disabilities.

Nouwen visited several L'Arche communities. Then, from 1 to 10 October 1985, whilst briefly visiting Toronto to serve as celebrant at a friend's wedding, he visited L'Arche Daybreak, the oldest and one of the largest L'Arche communities in North America/Canada. In his *Road to Daybreak*, written during the year in which he made his transition from scholar to carer, he prophesies:

> In my nine days at Daybreak I came to feel intimately a part of the intense joys and sorrows of this community of care. I have a deep love for the handicapped men and women and their assistants, who all received me with such warm hospitality. They did not hide anything from me. They allowed me to see their fears and their love. I feel deeply grateful for having been part of it all. I know that these days will deeply affect not only my time in France but also my decisions about the years to come.[31]

Those nine days were certainly going to affect Nouwen's time in France and, not only the years to come, but, indeed, for the remainder of his life. Nouwen and L'Arche proved to be mutually transformative. 'It was no surprise that he quickly identified with the wounded, as he was wounded and handicapped himself,' says Carolyn Whitney-Brown, a member of staff at Daybreak. 'He craved affirmation,' she continues, 'the knowledge that he was loved for who he was and not for what he *did*, not for what he *wrote*.' She concludes, 'Daybreak offered him an unconditional love that he would have found nowhere else.'[32] Vanier perceptively comments: 'He would have lost himself if he had stayed at Harvard or Yale, but he found himself in L'Arche.'[33]

During his days there, an accident, involving Ray, one of the core members, occurred. Perceiving how devastated everyone was by this crisis, Joe Egan invited Nouwen to offer his services as pastor and he restored peace and calm to both the core member's family (who, on seeing their son on the point of death, had begun to blame Daybreak for what had happened) and the community. Nouwen was warmly received and at the end of his stay felt very much part of the community there.

On 12 December 1985, Nouwen received a long letter from Egan on behalf of the Daybreak Community Council. They had been moved by the way in which Nouwen had ministered to them, and invited him to join the Daybreak community, serving as their pastor, and identifying the mutual blessing that could ensue:

> We truly feel that you have a gift to bring us. At the same time, our sense is that Daybreak would be a good place for you, too. We would want to support you in your important vocation of writing and speaking by providing you with a community that will love you and call you to grow.[34]

Nouwen regarded this as a divine call. Nouwen reflects:

> I am deeply moved by this letter. It is the first time in my life that I have
> been explicitly called ... Now a community is saying, 'We call you to live
> with us; to give to us and receive from us.' I know that Joe's invitation is
> not a job offer but a genuine call to come and live with the poor. They
> have no money to offer, no attractive living quarters, no prestige. This
> is a completely new thing. It is a concrete call to follow Christ, to leave
> the world of success, accomplishment, and honor, and to trust Jesus
> and him alone.[35]

No one had called Nouwen to a job in the same way before. He wisely sought
the advice of Vanier, Père Thomas (1905-93) – a Dominican priest who,
having spent some time as Vanier's spiritual mentor in Paris during the latter's
studies, had sown the idea of L'Arche in Vanier's mind – and others in the
L'Arche community and the approval of his own bishop. When Nouwen
had been in Trosly-Breuil, Père Thomas had taught him that 'very small
children have a deep, intuitive knowledge of God, a knowledge of the heart
that, sadly, is often obscured and even suffocated by the many systems of
thought we gradually acquire.'[36] Nouwen was soon to learn that 'Handicapped
people, who have such a limited ability to learn, can let their heart speak
easily and thus reveal a mystical life that for many intelligent people seems
unreachable.'[37] It was the people with learning disabilities, then, who taught
Nouwen that, for them at least, it was not so much a matter of embracing an
elaborate theology but the daily living out of a compassionate life that enabled
a knowledge of God, a knowledge of the heart, and a way of uniting them.

During his year at Trosly-Breuil, Nouwen was invited to write on a subject
that came to fruition during his breakdown. This was *Heart Speaks to Heart*,
a series of three gospel meditations on Jesus, which throws a great deal of
light on his spirituality during this period.[38]

Heart Speaks to Heart is not 'a contemporary interpretation of the devotion
to the Sacred Heart'[39] written at the behest of one Roman Catholic for other
Roman Catholics. It is, rather, a collection of simple prayers during the
writing of which Nouwen was led closer to the heart of Jesus. He ends the
book with the words: 'I hope and pray that all who will pray these prayers
with us will also experience the healing and renewing love that flows from
the heart of Jesus.'[40]

On 4 January 1986, Cardinal Simonis told Nouwen to go to Daybreak,
initially for three years, after which the option should remain open for
Nouwen to return to the Netherlands, if he so wished. In May 1986 Nouwen
visited Daybreak to meet with the L'Arche council there, who invited him to

tell them more about his spiritual journey and reasons for accepting their call to be pastor. Nouwen was asked to open a small spiritual centre called Dayspring as a source of spiritual renewal for the English-speaking L'Arche members and their families and friends, an inter-religious and multi-cultural place of renewal, mirroring the character of Toronto itself.

Nouwen, then, found himself at Daybreak, the oldest and one of the largest L'Arche communities in Canada/North America, in August 1986. At that time there were eighty people living in three houses on a farm thirty minutes from downtown Toronto. There were three more houses in the suburban town of Richmond Hill and a further two in Toronto. It was a community of people with different religions, backgrounds, lifestyles. Not everyone was a Christian and living in such a place called Nouwen to be a witness to God in a completely new way. He had described his spiritual journey there – as a kind of homecoming – during the previous months in *The Road to Daybreak*.[41] He was to provide for the spiritual needs of Evangelical, Protestant and Roman Catholic members, with and without learning disabilities, living in community there,[42] and he was to discover that L'Arche was the kind of community he had been looking for throughout his adult life. In his acceptance speech after receiving an honorary doctorate from Catholic Theological Union, Nouwen spoke these words:

> After twenty years in teaching, I felt a strong desire to live in community and to be close to those who are marginal in society. People with handicaps teach me that being is more important than doing, the heart is more important than the mind, and caring together is better than caring alone.[43]

One of the six people in the house where Nouwen was living was Adam Arnett (1961-96), a twenty-five year-old who needed total care. Nouwen was to have special responsibility for Adam and Adam was to be the subject of some articles and a later book, *Adam*.[44]

In compassionately following Jesus, Nouwen provoked a hostile reaction in some quarters. Following a Lent talk Nouwen had been invited to give in Cambridge, Massachusetts:

> People walked out [of St Paul's Church, Harvard Square, Massachusetts] asking how this great intellect, this former professor, could say he's learning from a man who can't even speak or walk. He got some hard letters from people and later said, 'I think if some of them had had stones they would have thrown them at me.'[45]

This was the first time Nouwen had been back to Massachusetts since joining L'Arche and the reception from many in the audience – full of some of the best brains from Yale, Harvard, Boston University and Massachusetts Institute of Technology – was less than complimentary. Many criticised Nouwen for moving from Harvard to L'Arche. One woman going so far as to write: 'Why are you living with those retarded people? They don't even understand you. People away from there need you much more.'[46]

Yet the vertiginous leap from Harvard to L'Arche, Daybreak, was crucial for Nouwen himself and, as we shall discover presently, offered a number of openings for both Nouwen and L'Arche, Daybreak. In the late 1980s Nouwen looked back to his time at Harvard and confessed: 'In the midst of this I kept on praying, "Lord, show me where you want me to go and I will follow you, but please be clear and unambiguous about it!" God was. Through Vanier God said, "Go and live among the poor in spirit, and they will heal you." The call was so clear and distinct that I had no choice but to follow.' So Nouwen moved from Harvard to L'Arche, from the brightest and best, to men and women who had few or no words and were considered marginal to the needs of our society. 'It was a very hard and painful move,' wrote Nouwen, a year or two later, 'and I am still in the process of making it.'[47]

In his *Road to Daybreak* (1988) Nouwen reflects: 'My decision to leave Harvard was a difficult one. For many months I was not sure if I would be following or betraying my vocation by leaving. The outer voices kept saying, "You can do so much good here. People need you!" The inner voices kept saying, "What good is it to preach the Gospel to others while losing your own soul?"' Then, in a perceptive piece of self-examination:

> Finally I realized that my increasing inner darkness, my feelings of being rejected by some of my students, colleagues, friends, and even God, my inordinate need for affirmation and affection, and my deep sense of not belonging were clear signs that I was not following the way of God's spirit. The fruits of the spirit are not sadness, loneliness, and separation, but joy, solitude, and community.[48]

Sr Sue Mosteller CSJ (1933-), in a recorded interview with Michael Ford, says that: 'For [Nouwen] to make the journey of his heart and come to live among us in L'Arche was very prophetic. Our society goes against such choices. People strive to get into universities, to make a name for themselves, to have status and success. He had that, but he chose another way.'[49]

Nouwen had spent some twenty years in the stimulating intellectual environment of academia. In coming to L'Arche, 'this little potato patch' as Sue describes it,[50] Nouwen was living out the gospel in all its fullness, its pain as well as its joy, with people who were a 'vehicle of love that we have neglected to observe.'[51] '[He] took up residence with a few people who had mental difficulties, who didn't know he had written a book and couldn't read it if they knew.'[52]

Writing in *Befriending Life*, Mary Bastedo (who was chair of the spiritual life committee at L'Arche Daybreak when Henri arrived) remarks that Nouwen's advent raised a few eyebrows: 'In September 1986, as I was pushing Adam Arnett in his wheelchair to the day program, a big yellow moving van full of Henri's possessions pulled in. Most assistants arrive with a backpack and a few possessions; here was a professor from Harvard arriving with all of this! Hence the raised eyebrows.'[53] Sue, who has been working at Daybreak since 1972, adds, 'It took him a while to get out of the classroom and just become Henri – friend, brother and pastor.'[54]

For the first fourteen months Nouwen was happy with his work but towards the end of 1987 he became severely depressed.[55] Coming as an Ivy League Professor, a Family Brother, a missionary, an internationally acclaimed speaker and writer, Nouwen came to care for people with learning disabilities and came to understand that he, himself, was wounded, vulnerable, estranged from himself – and God – and in 1988 suffered a severe nervous breakdown. Michael Ford depicts how:

> L'Arche was confronting [Henri] increasingly with his own wounds. And the sight scared him. In his words, it was as though the planks which had covered his emotional abyss had been taken away and he was staring into a canyon of wild animals waiting to devour him.[56]

The fact that Nouwen's handicaps were less visible than those of Adam and his fellow core members certainly didn't make them any less real.

Nouwen went to a retreat centre in Winnipeg, Manitoba, from January to July 1988, where he came under the guidance of two experienced spiritual directors. Throughout this period, Nouwen did not lose the gift or practice of writing and no less than three books were written, in which is described his spiritual struggle throughout the 'dark night of the soul', or as Bart Gavigan, the filmmaker, writer and lecturer,[57] has portrayed, the 'dark night of everything' – 'and it was very, very dark indeed.' The three books are *The Return of the Prodigal Son*, *Home Tonight*, and *The Inner Voice of Love*.

After recovering from his breakdown, Nouwen was able to help others, both inside and outside L'Arche. Michael Ford comments: 'The sun was rising on a whole new landscape for him. It wasn't simply a movement towards cross-cultural thinking, but a commitment to the life of the Beatitudes: "blessed are the poor.'"[58] As Vanier writes: 'He helped people to find themselves, to discover a vision'.[59]

Returning to L'Arche he embraces Daybreak, and, in the autumn of 1988, Nouwen increasingly emphasised the importance of grounding oneself in the love of God. This was, for him, a real home-coming. Back sharing his life in community with people with and without learning disabilities, he could later write in his diary with conviction, 'I am so truly convinced that the Spirit of God is present in our midst and that each person can be touched by God's Spirit in ways far beyond my own comprehension and intention.'[60]

Yet, out of this episode arose a certain degree of resolution. In the past, Nouwen had used his own vulnerability, his own wounded-ness, to enter into the vulnerability and wounded-ness of others, had connected and, employing insights acquired through his psycho-spiritual training, had started the healing process. Now, in returning to L'Arche Daybreak, he was even more aware of the need for compassionate living and was certain of the community, fellowship, and unity that could arise out of such compassionate living. He returned to L'Arche a more compassionate man; in both worship and in everyday activity, compassion was reaching its apotheosis. His teaching on compassion, inter-personal relationships, and unity were transformed from theory into reality.

In 1990 Vanier came to visit the community to evaluate all that had happened since Nouwen had joined. By then Vanier had become, according to Peter Weiskel (who had visited Nouwen at Trosly-Breuil), like an older brother in Christ to Nouwen, and Nouwen had experienced at first hand the nature and nurture of compassion in action.

Nouwen returns to consider aspects of compassion, and in particular that of discipleship, in his *Here and Now: Living in the Spirit*, published in 1994, that is to say, some twenty years after working on *Compassion* and a couple of years before his death. It is the fruit of his years spent at L'Arche Daybreak. Here, Nouwen asks, 'What does it mean to live in the world with a truly compassionate heart, a heart that remains open to all people at all times?' He continues, 'It is very important to realize that compassion is more than sympathy or empathy.'[61] Christians are told to be compassionate, as our Father is. We are encouraged to root that compassion in prayer, to depend on God and others, and to seek solitude. All are to accept divine love, freely given to us by the One who calls us to compassion. We are to eschew competition, to discover what we hold in common with others, to be aware of the need for compassion in our living day-to-day, to enter into a fellowship with the weak. As Michael Higgins has written, 'the mark of friendship is co-sympathy, that to be present for another in pain is to be present in that other's pain. This is genuine compassion: to suffer with another is love. It is to be Jesus.'[62]

Our problem, the writers of *Compassion* state, is that we are compelled to recognise competition, not compassion, as our main motivation in life. 'We define ourselves in ways that require us to maintain distance from one another.'[63] This competition, this distancing, 'reaches into the smallest corners of our relationships, prevents us from entering into full solidarity with each other, and stands in the way of our being compassionate. We all too often forget that "He has embraced everything human with the infinite tenderness of his compassion".'[64] 'We prefer to keep compassion on the periphery of our competitive lives. Being compassionate would require giving up dividing lines and relinquishing differences ... distinctions and ... losing our identities ... This fear ... makes us into competitive people who compulsively cling to our differences and defend them at all cost, even to the point of violence.'[65] Human compassion, then, because of its competitive element may be strongly contrasted with divine compassion, which has no degree of competition. God is not in competition with us and, therefore, only God may be totally compassionate.

Nouwen had been afforded a sabbatical from L'Arche Daybreak from 2 September 1995, to 30 August 1996, with the mandate not to do any work except for writing. During this time he kept an extensive journal, running to almost 700 pages in manuscript,[66] which was to become *Sabbatical Journey: The Diary of His Final Year*, his last book.

For the first four months of Nouwen's writing sabbatical he lived in Watertown, six miles north-west of Boston. During these months, at the beginning of November 1995, Nouwen journeyed from Watertown to Cancún, Mexico, to address The Gathering, a three-day meeting held annually to enable an evangelical support network for philanthropists (each of which is a major donor to a charitable organisation), who still come together to discuss how to give in the spirit of the gospel. On 1 November 1995, Nouwen notes, 'Most important for me is that I can speak as a member of a community where the poor form the center.'[67] The poor he writes about are the core members of L'Arche.

Nouwen begins his entry for 10 November, 'As I started to write today, I realized that The Gathering had raised new questions in my mind about mission, evangelization, conversion, witness, and so on. Many of the people I met in Cancún believe that without an explicit personal profession of faith in Jesus as our Lord and Savior, we cannot make it to heaven. They are convinced that God has called us to convert every human being to Jesus.'[68] He continues, 'This vision inspires much generosity, commitment, and a great world-wide project,' but some lines further on he reflects, 'Still ... I felt somewhat uncomfortable, even though this belief was present in my own upbringing.'[69] And, then, Nouwen makes a proclamation that flies completely in the face of what we might expect from him: 'My conviction as a young man was that there is no salvation outside the Catholic Church and that it was my task to bring all "non believers" into the one true church.'[70]

The chapter ends with a section sketching Nouwen's final years shared with people with and without learning disabilities at L'Arche, where, through his abundant friendships, charismatic teaching and prolific writing, he opened up to an ever widening network of people from various faiths and none.

Recording his thoughts on 10 November 1995, as he journeyed back from Mexico to Boston, Henri Nouwen's entry in his final diary seems to be nothing less than a summation of what he has to say on evangelisation, mission, re-integration, salvation, and unity. As the Catholic Church opened its doors to non-Catholic observers and commentators at Vatican II, and published *Unitatis Redintegratio* (The Decree on Ecumenism, 1964), there was a very real sense in which Christians of all denominations and, indeed, all human beings – *whether they know about Jesus or not* – could walk through the door to God's house:

> Much has happened to me over the years. My own psychological training, my exposure to people from the most different religious backgrounds, the Second Vatican Council, the new theology of mission, and my life in L'Arche have all deepened and broadened my views on Jesus' saving work. Today I personally believe that while Jesus came to open the door to God's house, all human beings can walk through that door, whether they know about Jesus or not. Today I see it as my call to help every person claim his or her own way to God. I feel deeply called to witness for Jesus as the one who is the source of my own spiritual journey and thus create the possibility for other people to know Jesus and commit themselves to him.[71]

'The further you descend, the more your eyes are opened to the brokenness of our humanity'

Nouwen saw Vanier as a kindred spirit, someone who had left a promising academic career to live and work with the poor and handicapped, moreover someone who was sharing in the work of retrieval.[72] Nouwen was to discover, through Vanier and L'Arche, the path that would eventually reveal the home he had been searching for in response to his belief that God had been calling him where he might serve the poor. Compassion, at last, fully in action. In 1983, following his tour of lecturing on Latin America, Nouwen stayed for six weeks at Trosly-Breuil. His first visit. Vanier neither asked Nouwen to present a lecture, nor did he invite him to write a book. He sensed that Nouwen was 'a man without a home',[73] and simply told him, 'We have a home for you and we really don't want you to do very much. Just waste some time with us!'[74] It was to be in this 'sharing' or simply 'being', rather than 'ministering to', where Nouwen was ultimately to discover the retrieval of 'an authentically Christian vision of the world.' The people at L'Arche encouraged him to pray, to go to the chapel alone, to sleep in, or have dinner with some of the core members in their homes.[75] Nouwen immediately felt at home:

> The non-competitive life with mentally handicapped people, their gifts of welcoming me regardless of name or prestige, and the persistent invitation to 'waste some time' with them opened in me a place that until then had remained unavailable to me, a place where I could hear the gentle invitation of Jesus to dwell with him.[76]

Here at last we find Henri Nouwen seeking compassion and ultimately finding and sharing a home with people with and without learning disabilities in L'Arche.

Even in the final decade of his life when he was living in L'Arche, Nouwen was compelled to face his shortcomings and, from a practical point of view, there were very many.

The challenge to gear down and relax into a slow-paced, simple domestic schedule was great. The impact of pastoral psychology on Nouwen's compassionate ministry in L'Arche was immense. Using the insights from his studies in pastoral psychology, Nouwen was now able to hold together the meeting points between God, the individual, and community. After recovering from his breakdown (1987-88), Nouwen was both the wounded minister and the healing minister, living day-to-day with folk in community where he was reawakening God's love in a world in which the marginalised were at the centre of things.

Nouwen showed that having opened oneself up to the possibility of displacement, *kenosis*, and downward mobility, one may discover a new awareness of resting in God, a new sense of homecoming, a new life shared with others, a new commonality, in which an authentically Christian vision of the world could be retrieved. Written during his year-long stay in Trosly-Breuil, Nouwen acknowledged that L'Arche was the main inspiration for the reflections in *In the House of the Lord* and that the titles of its three sections – intimacy, fecundity and ecstasy – were given him by Vanier. Vanier had said that, 'Working with mentally handicapped people, I have come to recognize that all human beings, whatever, their condition, are called to intimacy, fecundity, and ecstasy.'[77] These three gifts may lead to a conversion in L'Arche for its core members and its assistants, in fact for all who live there and indeed, as L'Arche may be perceived as a microcosm of the world, for all created beings, offering conversion, development, and downward growth in Jesus.[78]

> It was in making the decision to go to Daybreak ... that Nouwen truly experienced the challenges inherent in what he was trying to say about compassion and caring.[79]

'I may say that the contrast between my university life and my life here in L'Arche is greater than I realized at the outset,' admits Nouwen. 'The contrast isn't so much between intelligent students and mentally handicapped people as in the "ascending" style of the university and the "descending" style of L'Arche.' Then he develops the idea of contrasting mobilities: 'You might say that at Yale and Harvard they're principally interested in upward mobility, whereas here they believe in the importance of downward mobility. That's the radical difference, and I notice in myself how difficult it is to change direction on the ladder.' Nouwen ends with a revelation: 'It has become very clear to me now that the further you descend, the more your eyes are opened to the brokenness of our humanity.'[80]

'We are guided by love on every step of our lives'

> When I joined the L'Arche Daybreak Community in Toronto, I was searching for a new home. I knew it could not be the old home that I had left, but I did not know what the new home would look like.[81]
>
> I have experienced much loneliness, much confusion, and much insecurity, but I have experienced all of this sorrow living with poor people who in their simplicity and openness offer me a space that gradually could become a new home.[82]

As Michael Higgins has succinctly worded it, 'Daybreak would be his Jerusalem; it is where he would find peace and a new level of suffering.'[83] It was to prove 'a place of very deep personal poverty' – his unresolved internal struggle with his sexual identity, his emotional dependency on the affirmation of others, the apparent silence of God, his rootlessness, his ever-decreasing feeling of self-worth – 'a place of breakdown'. Nouwen was 'on the fast track to a psychic collapse.'[84] Nevertheless, it was also to prove a place of healing and to provide the welcoming community that Nouwen so badly needed.

Nouwen's time spent at the Abbey of the Genesee, although influential in opening him up to the monastic life, especially the significance of contemplation, and nurturing his desire for community, both important for developing his understanding of compassion, as we have seen, was not the place for him to stay.

Similarly, though Latin America had taught Nouwen 'something of the reciprocity of missionary work, the graced mutuality that defines effective evangelizing,'[85] it was clear that Nouwen received more from the poor in the way of companionship than they received, in terms of his learning or psychological expertise, from him. The *barrio*, like the churches of the Netherlands, and the silence of the cloister, proved no place for Nouwen.

Nouwen's years of lecturing at Harvard, being the locus if not the cause of his pain, had shown him – with an increasing feeling of dislocation – that, for Nouwen, there was no place for the heart in the contemporary university, despite offering, and fulfilling, opportunities for ecumenism, and, therefore, there was no place for him, or his teaching, either in style or in content. 'Harvard came to represent for him the pinnacle of university arrogance, its undiluted focus on achievement the death knell of the soul.'[86]

When, therefore, Nouwen was invited to live and care at Daybreak, it meant that 'he could move from the infelicitous House of Fear to the welcoming House of Love; living among those he called "the true barometers of the spirit," he could find the joy, the intimacy, and the ecstasy that had eluded him for so many years.'[87] The time when 'the thorn in his flesh had become even more painful,' as Laurent had expressed these years for his brother in the early 1980s, was over.[88] At last, his aching to integrate with others in community was starting to receive healing. And Nouwen and L'Arche were to teach one another about the welcoming and hospitality that enable and nourish compassion.

> In coming to L'Arche, Nouwen was to learn at first-hand what caring entailed. He was to experience what it is to be vulnerable. He was to earth, to make real, all that he had learnt and taught about pastoral psychology and compassion. He was to experience ecumenism and inter-faith dialogue in new and creative ways. And all of this brought an extra maturity to his writing.[89] Communion creates community, because the God living in us makes us recognize the God in our fellow humans.[90]

Although open to those of other faiths, Nouwen's writings are essentially Christian, and it is here that he can cross boundaries of traditions, without diluting his own. At the same time, he never advocates a rootless spirituality that can call no place home. Quite the opposite. Roman Catholic, Nouwen believed profoundly that he had much to offer to Protestants and knew that they, also, had much to offer him. As Nouwen, McNeill, and Morrison had written in *Compassion*, 'In the community gathered in Christ's name, there is an unlimited space into which strangers from different places with very different stories can enter and experience God's compassionate presence.'[91]

Michael Ford describes in his *Wounded Prophet* a rare instance of a Jew frequently receiving communion at Nouwen's altar:

> One of Nouwen's students at Yale was a young Jew called Dean Hammer who became a ploughshares activist in 1980 ... After leaving the Divinity School, Hammer had helped develop the Covenant Peace Community in New Haven, which Nouwen supported in various ways, including celebrating the Eucharist on Friday mornings ... Nouwen's theology and practice of the Eucharist became a centre-piece in Hammer's life: 'I was raised in the synagogue and in the Jewish tradition – but it was through Henri and participating in his Eucharists that I came to believe that, even as a Jew, I belonged round the table.'[92]

Nouwen records his thoughts on leaving academia and journeying towards community in his diary *The Road to Daybreak: A Spiritual Journey* covering the months August 1985 to July 1986 (published 1988). Here he describes the move to Daybreak as a kind of homecoming. At L'Arche Daybreak he found the type of community that he had been searching for. Living in one of the homes, he was asked to care for Adam Arnett, a young man with profound learning disabilities. Nouwen's *Adam: God's Beloved* (written 1996, completed by Sue Mosteller and published 1997) describes how Adam became his friend and teacher, truly learning from the vulnerable and wounded. During his breakdown Nouwen wrote a series of notes to himself, which he called spiritual imperatives, full of lessons learnt from pastoral psychology. These were published some years later, at the continued insistence of his friends, as *The Inner Voice of Love: A Journey from Anguish to Freedom* (written 1988, published on the day of his death in 1996).

Adam could not speak and rarely smiled. He was, of all the core members, the most compromised, the most damaged, the most in need of care, and this was the young man whom Joe Egan,[93] the community leader at the time, chose for Nouwen to care for. Nouwen was to be Adam's reference person, his key assistant. 'It was with some trepidation,' Ford writes, 'that the community assigned [Henri] to Adam.' 'It was Henri's calvary moment.'[94] Like most assistants, Nouwen began by watching other people on the spot but he picked his job up quickly. With Adam he was very comfortable and he did his work very faithfully. Moreover, as Nouwen records, Adam seemed to call Nouwen 'back to stillness at the eye of the cyclone'.

Jean Vanier comments: 'Henri's life was touched and changed because of his friendship with Adam Arnett ... By coming to understand Adam, he experienced how the world is upside down in its quest for fame, fortune, and power.'[95]

Nouwen himself, in an early article on Adam,[96] describes how 'this deeply handicapped young man, who is considered by many outsiders a vegetable, a distortion of humanity, a useless animal-like creature who shouldn't have been born' showed him how to pray, 'teaching me what no book, school or professor could ever teach me': 'Ever since I've been praying with Adam I've known better than before that praying is being with Jesus, simply "wasting time" with him. Adam keeps teaching me that'.

In his book on the French philosopher and Christian existentialist, Gabriel Marcel (1889-1973), Paul Marcus singles out Nouwen for his 'being with,' rather than 'ministering to,' core members in L'Arche:

> There was Henry (sic) Nouwen, a Harvard, Yale, and Notre Dame professor (and also a Dutch-born Catholic priest), finding his greatest contentment and instruction being with (not 'ministering' to, which is very different) the mentally challenged at L'Arche Community in France and Canada.[97]

Nathan Ball, in an interview with Higgins, goes further and says, 'Henri was a man of remarkable compassion ... his ability to communicate the dynamics of such compassion was extraordinary. Henri became a font of compassion for Adam, his immediate family, the members of his house, and the Daybreak community itself.'[98]

In a published interview with Gunar Kravalis, then minister of St Andrew's Presbyterian Church in Aurora, Ontario, Nouwen repeated that Adam constantly reminded him that: 'What makes us human is not the mind, but the heart, not our ability to think, but our ability to love.'[99] And, again: 'The heart allows us to become sons and daughters of God and brothers and sisters of each other. Long before the mind is able to exercise its power, the heart is already able to develop a trusting human relationship'[100] with all people, in all places, and at all times.

Whilst he was at L'Arche, Nouwen wrote fourteen books,[101] including, arguably, his most popular work, *The Return of the Prodigal Son: A Story of Homecoming* (written 1988, published 1992).

> I know that living with the people of my community is calling me to be a witness in a way that I never could have been before.[102]

Ford records Nouwen telling him that when he returned to L'Arche, after his months of therapy – 'a hugely painful and an immensely healing time' – his 'conflicting struggles and feelings of rejection could be transformed by enabling him to be a more compassionate priest.'[103] He gradually became the father in more than simply title, and daily and liturgical life at Daybreak developed as a consequence.

Returning to L'Arche Daybreak in the autumn of 1988, Nouwen increasingly emphasised the importance of grounding oneself in the love of God, and the importance of self-giving. In this grounding, which was daily lived out at Daybreak, Nouwen became more relaxed and his own spirituality grew in inner peace.

Then, in *Life of the Beloved*, Nouwen articulated something new, something holistic and transforming. He argued that, just as Jesus took, blessed, broke and gave bread, so Christ, also, was similarly taken, blessed by God at His baptism, broken on the cross, and then given to the world. And, in the same way that our Lord was taken, blessed, broken and given, people, too, are taken ('everyone who believes is first "chosen" by God, and placed in their unique circumstances in life'[104]), blessed ('a blessing is pure affirmation, and it empowers. The blessing of God reveals a [person's] true nature as [a daughter] or [a son of God]'[105]), broken ('like Jesus, [a person is] also "broken" by life's sorrows'[106]), and given ('the result of [a person] being broken is that, again like Jesus, [that person is] "given" to the world. [people's] lives are a gift'[107]). Nouwen summarises:

> To identify the movements of the Spirit in our lives, I have found it helpful to use four words: taken, blessed, broken and given ... these words summarize my life as a priest ... [they] also summarize my life as a Christian ... most importantly, however, they summarize my life as a human being because in every moment of my life somewhere, somehow the taking, the blessing, the breaking and the giving are happening.[108]

Vanier sums up the mutual transformation of Nouwen and L'Arche Daybreak: 'Henri was a gift to the Daybreak community and his friends at Daybreak continually inspired and refreshed him,'[109] a point endorsed by Mary Bastedo who states, 'Daybreak helped Henri to make a passage of personal growth and to discover a great fruitfulness in the last ten years of his life. Henri helped Daybreak to make a passage into spiritual maturity and a dynamic sense of mission. This mutual transformation created a legacy to be shared, a treasure for which we are now taking responsibility.'[110]

The final part of the eighth chapter of *Compassion* is given over to reflecting on the breaking of the bread. 'Prayer', Nouwen and his co-writers state, 'finds its most profound expression in the breaking of the bread ... it stands at the center of the Christian community. In the breaking of the bread together, we give the clearest testimony to the communal character of our prayers ...

It is in the breaking of the bread together that the Holy Spirit becomes most tangibly present to the community ... The breaking of the bread ... is ...the festive articulation of what we perceive as the center of our lives.'[111] This is unpacked when we read:

> When we eat bread and drink wine together in memory of Christ, we become intimately related to his own compassionate life. In fact, we *become* his life and are thus enabled to re-present Christ's life in our time and place. Our compassion becomes a manifestation of God's compassion lived out through all times and in all ages. The breaking of the bread connects our broken lives with God's life in Christ and transforms our brokenness into a brokenness that no longer leads to fragmentation but to community and love.[112]

In this way, praying together becomes a working together, and the invitation to break bread becomes an invitation to action.

Nouwen encountered Christ most fully in the Eucharist and in his teaching of the parallels between the taking, blessing, breaking and giving of Jesus and of other people, a shatteringly new concept in Nouwen's thinking bursts forth from this period. It is in Nouwen's *Life of the Beloved* that he begins systematically to address the lesson of taking, blessing, breaking and giving, which he learnt in L'Arche, to the world. The book was written at the invitation of Fred Bratman, a secular Jewish friend from Nouwen's Yale years. Intended not as a religious but as a spiritual book for Fred and his friends, people who had little to do (so they thought) with Jesus, its teaching that everyone is connected with Jesus became a universal paradigm for all the Fred Bratmans of this world. It is this lesson that prepares a person to stand alongside their fellow human beings as children of God, as brothers and sisters, and, in so doing, enter into a deeper communion both with God and one another.

'In and through God', Nouwen professes, 'we can be faithful to each other: in friendship, marriage, and community. This intimate bond with God, constantly nurtured by prayer, offers us a true home. We can live together in this home without asking for much more than a willingness to constantly confess our weaknesses to each other and to always forgive each other.'[113] Nouwen comments that Vanier considered this divine covenant to be the basis of every form of human faithfulness, and argued that people can only stay together when the 'staying power' comes from the One who comes to stay with them. 'When we know ourselves to be deeply anchored in that divine covenant, we can build homes together. Only then can our limited and broken love reflect the unlimited and unbroken love of God.'[114]

> The intimacy of the house of love always leads to solidarity with the weak. The closer we come to the heart of the One who loves us with an unconditional love, the closer we come to each other in the solidarity of a redeemed humanity.[115]

There is an important passage in *In the House of the Lord* in which Nouwen reflects on divine love. He points out that when St John writes that fear is driven out by love, he is pointing to a love that comes from God, a divine love. St John, he argues, is not writing about human affection, mutual attraction, psychological compatibility, or deep interpersonal feelings, important though these are. Divine love, the love about which St John writes, embraces and transcends every emotion, feeling, and passion, driving out all fear, and it is this divine love in which the human family is invited to participate. The home, the place of intimacy, the place of real belonging, is, then, not a place constructed by human hands. 'It is fashioned for us by God, who came to pitch his tent among us, invite us to his place, and prepare a room for us in his own house.'[116]

In an open letter from Trosly-Breuil written in 1990, Vanier writes, '[Nouwen] became very important to L'Arche. First of all, he understood L'Arche, as he showed especially in the book *Adam: God's Beloved*.[117] 'When I pray,' Nouwen professes, 'I enter into the depth of my own heart and find there the heart of God, who speaks to me of love. And I recognize, right there, the place where all of my sisters and brothers are in communion with one another.'[118] It is these lessons about contemplation, about communion, and about solidarity, that make *Heart Speaks to Heart* arguably the most universal of all Nouwen's books. Its insights appear to inspire Nouwen in his final years to palpably live, work, and worship compassionately.

Nouwen urges his readers to 'dare to reclaim the truth that we are God's chosen ones.'[119] This is no competitive or individualistic claim. In reclaiming 'chosen-ness' a person cannot but help to realise and accept the uniqueness of others as Beloved of God, not suppressing opposites but welcoming the stranger. It is, in fact, a compassionate claim. Nouwen teaches his readers to 'keep unmasking the world about [us] for what it is: manipulative, controlling, power-hungry and, in the long run, destructive.'[120] He also encourages his readers to 'keep looking for people and places where [our] truth is spoken and where [we] are reminded of our deepest identity as the chosen one.'[121] And people are encouraged to 'celebrate [our] chosen-ness constantly.'[122]

However, it is not enough to be chosen, Nouwen points out:

The blessings that we give to each other are expressions of the blessing that rests on us from all eternity. It is the deepest affirmation of our true self. It is not enough to be chosen. We also need an ongoing blessing that allows us to hear in an ever-new way that we belong to a loving God who will never leave us alone, but will remind us always that we are guided by love on every step of our lives.[123]

It is these reassuring words, that each person belongs to an ever present, loving God, who accompanies them 'every step of the way', that enables a holistic and transforming way of life.

At L'Arche Nouwen, as we have already seen, found a home. Once he had set aside the desire to find new people and experiences to fill and satiate himself, the deeper the simple vulnerability and love of the core members penetrated and transformed him. Some years previously at Yale Nouwen had written with other Roman Catholics about compassion. Now recovering from his breakdown, he learnt the lesson of mutuality and interdependence, an 'exquisite reciprocity',[124] not only between himself and his new family but also the one between himself and Christ, and this lesson, once learnt, was to colour much of his final years and writing. As he writes in *Our Greatest Gift*, we are, 'children of God, brothers and sisters of each other and parents of the generations to come.'[125]

'Let us pray that each of our communities will be in solidarity with those who suffer, and be a place of hope in a world of divisions and despair'

As a carer, as I have noted, Nouwen had special responsibility for Adam Arnett, as revealed in *Adam: God's Beloved*, and Adam's life may stand as an example of a transformed and transforming life. Nouwen believed that Adam, like Jesus, had been sent into the world to fulfil a unique mission not in action but in passion. Adam was not fully recognised in his church and it was painful for his parents when they learned that because of his handicap Adam could not receive Confirmation and the sacraments of Eucharist with the other children of his age. Later, however, in a small faith-sharing group, Adam made his First Communion and celebrated with this small community of friends. Adam's funeral took place on Thursday, 15 February 1996, with a few hundred people gathered in St Mary Immaculate Roman Catholic Church in Richmond Hill.

Standing in front of Adam's body, holding the Eucharistic bread and speaking Jesus' words, 'Take and eat, this is my Body given for you', I knew in a whole new way that God has become body for us so that we can touch God and be healed. God's body and Adam's body are one, because, Jesus tells us clearly, 'Insofar as you did this to one of the least of these brothers of mine, you did it to me' (Mt 25:40). In Adam, indeed, we touched the living Christ among us.

Everyone came to the front of the church to receive the Body of Christ, and – after the Eucharist – everyone came again to touch Adam's coffin as a last farewell.[126]

Nathan Ball reflects, 'Henri was the catalyst for this quality of caring and compassion that is, in my experience, very rare ... His gift to the world in general and in particular to the people who were in his life, was his ability to be a compassionate and transformative presence. His attending to Adam during his dying is the master expression of this gift.'[127]

Ball explains how Henri 'would come daily to the hospital and infuse the place with a pastoral presence and care that was profoundly healing. His love, energy, and focus drew people together in a way that allowed them to see the sacredness of the moment; he provided a unity built on our ability to celebrate the gift of Adam's life even in the midst of a painful sadness.'[128]

Having written what virtually amounted to his own creed (*Bread for the Journey*), Nouwen thought of writing a book on the Apostles' Creed but following Adam's death in February 1996, he changed his mind and decided, instead, to write what Adam's life had taught him about the Christian life. Nouwen died before this was brought to completion and Sue Mosteller, Nouwen's colleague, and literary executrix, who became Director of the Henri Nouwen Literary Center, finished both this and the *Sabbatical Journey* and saw them through the press.

The fruits of Nouwen's spiritual development through living at Daybreak have proved a lasting legacy. Bastedo comments on how the realisation of a holistic and transforming way of life contributed not only to L'Arche but also to ecumenism and inter-faith dialogue: 'Today important elements of Henri's vision and practice continue to shape our life together and, I believe, are prophetic not just for Daybreak but for the many communities of L'Arche around the world and for countless other faith communities.'[129] She lists three qualities of Nouwen's ministry that she finds have been transforming for her: inclusivity; intimacy; and speaking inspirationally about the gift that the poor or marginalised can offer. On the subject of inclusivity she comments: 'This is the quality of Henri's ministry that most remains with me. He was ecumenical in the true sense of the word. Henri used a language that not only was inclusive of both men and women but was simple and contemporary, cutting across denominational boundaries and intellectual differences.'

Nouwen's inclusivity was not only a cerebral matter. 'His liturgical practice was also inclusive: having everyone sit in a circle, welcoming guests, offering the Eucharist to all those who in good conscience felt called to receive it, and blessing those who chose not to receive.' Then, in an all too rare remark about Nouwen and interfaith dialogue, she continues: 'Likewise, Henri sensitively welcomed those of other faiths who occasionally visited, and the community began to develop interfaith friendships. He lived his priesthood not as something that excluded others but rather as a way to invite others into participation.'

Mary Bastedo confesses how she had been challenged and transformed by Nouwen's approach to community: 'Henri was very attentive to individuals in their personal journeys, encouraging them in their struggles. He could raise questions without being judgmental. He was able to live with the gray. This quality challenged me.' Looking back, she reflects, 'As the community leader of a small community, I had been accustomed to making clear-cut decisions. I was more black-and-white about what was acceptable in community life.' Now, transformed, she discovers a new way of living and gains in confidence: 'Yet I saw the fruitfulness of Henri's approach, saw people finding and growing in faith and making commitments in the light of faith. I saw the vitality of a community that was able to embrace diversity and encourage creativity. I was challenged to stretch my boundaries and to live with the gray.'[130]

Bastedo also comments on how Nouwen taught by example on intimacy: 'Henri always struggled with intimacy: yet he was able to achieve it, especially in his capacity to move in close to those who were suffering.' She then refers back to the first encounter Daybreak had with Nouwen: 'We witnessed this with Raymond and his family after the car accident and we saw it repeatedly. Henri taught the community a lot about compassionate presence to those who are suffering and, especially, to those who are dying.' She concludes: 'All that we learned was preparation for Henri's own death, when we held a wake and an all-night vigil and organised a three-hour funeral celebration.'[131]

And on the gift of L'Arche, Bastedo writes: 'For years before Henri arrived, Sue Mosteller had been saying, "L'Arche is about much more than living in a home with people who have a disability."' With the advent of Nouwen, L'Arche, too, was enabled to articulate something of the gift that L'Arche offers to the world: 'Henri's coming to Daybreak helped us find the words to express what L'Arche is and share it with a much wider circle. Today we speak of L'Arche as a school of the heart, where we learn the values of hospitality, compassion, forgiveness, and mutual relationship; a place where we discover that the apparently poor person has much to give others.' She concludes: '[L'Arche is]a place where we get in touch with our own poverty and limits and find God's presence in our weakness a place where we learn to know who God is as a lover and friend.'[132]

Bert Witvoet, then journalist on *Calvinist Contact*, gives two insights into everyday life at L'Arche, Daybreak:

> In this silent room (the Daybreak chapel) some 12 of us quieted [sic] down and read scripture. Henri delivered a beautiful sermonette about focusing your activity, doing what you must do and then leaving, like the disciples had to do when entering and leaving cities. We prayed communally, tasted the bread and wine, which was celebrated in a simple, ecumenical way. I could almost touch the peace that Henri had described in talking about Adam.
>
> This sense of peace was further confirmed when I had lunch with assistants and handicapped people ... it was all so down-to-earth and so much like the incarnation of Christ: Immanuel – God in the flesh.[133]

I have referred to Vanier's open letter from Trosly written in 1990. It continues: 'Also, he had what I call the sacrament of the word. He knew how to say things that people would listen to and had a power of the word, especially the written word.'[134] Nouwen was a welcoming preacher, an intelligible lecturer, an impassioned public speaker, and an accessible communicator, speaking and writing in a language that was not his mother tongue. Lorenzo Sforza-Cesarini, an assistant at the Woodery, in a recorded interview with Michael Ford recalls: '[Nouwen] had a very strong way of delivering the message of Jesus from his own knowledge, and somehow by his enthusiasm he was able to capture people's minds and hearts. You might not remember his words – but the Spirit was visible in what happened between him and individuals, or a group of people.'[135]

The learning process was two-way and both Nouwen and L'Arche grew through it: 'In the end a simpler life with simpler people was richer and more satisfying than Ivy League academia or any of the options he had tried, because God's kingdom is revealed to such as these.'[136]

Mary Bastedo recognises three elements that enabled the transformation of Daybreak and other L'Arche communities: inclusivity: intimacy; and the teaching of L'Arche itself, on compassion, forgiveness, hospitality, and reciprocal relationship: 'He claimed his spiritual fatherhood and nourished the community by word and sacrament. He was Daybreak's first full-time priest and brought a whole new vision for L'Arche in North America.'[137]

Bastedo describes how L'Arche Daybreak shared its compassionate way of living and connected with the world outside: 'Henri helped us have confidence that we do have something to say to the world around us. The new Dayspring chapel, which was Henri's dream and for which he raised most of the funds, was completed in January 1999,' that is, three years after Nouwen's passing. She continues, 'It has become a place where community members are being empowered to share about their lives and thus enable many more people to experience our spirituality. Every week high school students come for retreat days, and many people from Toronto and afar participate in periodic days of reflection offered by the community.' A year earlier Daybreak had asked Bastedo to explore a ministry to families who have a child with a disability living at home. 'Several of these families now come to our weekly community worship. Faith and Light support groups for persons who have disabilities, their families, and young volunteers have also sprung from this work,'[138] she explains.

In most L'Arche houses and communities foot-washing took place, notably as part of the Maundy Thursday liturgy, and this acquired a special significance when people from divided Churches came to worship together. Sue Mosteller, in a private communication, informs me that the practice of foot-washing began at a Covenant Retreat with Jean Vanier in India - where a common closing ceremony was wanted - and could not be the Eucharist or something totally Christian. She adds that it would have been in the early 1980s. Nouwen refers to it in *The Road to Daybreak*.[139]

> Every Holy Thursday, it was our ritual to have the Washing of the Feet, together with the whole community gathered. [Henri] LOVED it and was totally IN it, giving himself to help us bless each other as we did the washing and as we were being washed.[140]

Towards the end of *In the House of the Lord* Nouwen draws our attention to the significance of L'Arche:

> L'Arche is certainly not a new international order, nor the end of wars and violence, nor the beginning of a new foreign policy. But it is a light 'put on the lamp stand where it shines for everyone in the house' (Matthew 5:15). Jean Vanier does not want the light of L'Arche kept under a basket.

Nouwen then quotes Vanier:

> We do not seek to have nice little warm communities which are cut off from the outside world. L'Arche participates in the struggle for justice; it wants to be in solidarity with the poor and oppressed all over the world; .

it wants to struggle for peace. But its way of doing all this is different from the ways of large political and social movements.

Here is a reality about retrieval in which sentimentality has no place:

> Our struggle is essentially a struggle for life. We want to affirm that the life of each human being, each person, is important particularly when that person is very poor, very diminished; we try to make this affirmation not by making speeches but by significant actions. ... At every moment, we need to struggle so that each one can find the security and the human presence alongside him or her which is needed to help him or her *want* to live and grow ...
>
> Sometimes we will only be able to be alongside them in heart and encouragement, but at other times we can occasionally bring an effective presence. Let us pray that each of our communities will be in solidarity with those who suffer, and be a place of hope in a world of divisions and despair. (*Letters of L'Arche*, September 1985, p. 1)[141]

Nouwen himself concludes:

> L'Arche reminds us that a worldwide movement of care for the poor and the oppressed can engender a new consciousness which transcends the boundaries of sex, religion, race, and nation. Such a consciousness can give birth to a world community, a community to celebrate our shared humanity, to sing a joyful song of praise to the God of love, and to proclaim the ultimate victory of life over death.[142]

Nouwen has been shown to call man back to himself in God, to his task of 'reincarnating God's love, mercy, and justice in the world,'[143] in ways that are pastorally effective and theologically sound. In this sense 'drawing His divided household back to one table' has referred not only to the centripetally ecumenical aspect of Nouwen's life and work but also to his drawing spirituality and psychology together into one cohesive means of ministry, in which the minister is, in turn, both wounded and healing, enabling students to 'connect the insights of modern psychology with spiritual practice and understanding,'[144] and addressing the basic human needs of core members and assistants alike at L'Arche Daybreak, leading towards feelings of compassion.

'During my time here at Daybreak, I have been led to an inner place where I had not been before. It is the place within me where God has chosen to dwell.'[145] A few lines later Nouwen admits, 'This place had always been there I had always been aware of it as the source of grace.'[146] After much displacement, self-emptying, and downward growth, Nouwen realises that 'I am called to enter into the inner sanctuary of my own being where God has chosen to dwell.'[147] He ends his Prologue with these words:

> The only way to that place is prayer, unceasing prayer. Many struggles and much pain can clear the way, but I am certain that only unceasing prayer can let me enter it.[148]

From this viewpoint Nouwen is called to 'see' 'an authentically Christian vision of the world,' as he puts it, 'looking at people and this world through the eyes of God.'[149] From this vantage point he is able to speak and write into his own and others' lives. Listening to 'the heartbeat of God,'[150] he can say what he hears. He is, he writes, 'well aware of the enormity of this vocation,' but is 'confident that it is the only way for me.'[151]

In his *Letters to Marc about Jesus*, written for his nephew on what it means to live a spiritual life, Nouwen reflects that it had become very clear to him that the further one descended, the more one's eyes were opened to the broken-ness of our humanity, and yet this descent, through solidarity, consolation, and comfort, could issue in an ascent to a new way of living. 'The descending way of love, the way to the poor, the broken and the oppressed becomes the ascending way of love, the way to joy and peace and new life.'[152]

Nouwen describes the global dimension of joy and ecstasy, calling for a new way of living as a consequence of resting in God, centring one's life on Jesus, discerning the gifts of the Holy Spirit, and discovering the divine in all:

> Joy is radically different from happiness, for it does not depend upon the 'ups' and 'downs' of our existence. It is the constant moving away from the static places of death toward the house of God, where the abundant life can be recognized and celebrated.
>
> Ecstasy, like intimacy and fecundity, has a global dimension. Seen in the context of a world on the verge of self-destruction, ecstasy calls for a new international order and invites the nations to view their separate identities not as a cause for war, but as unique contributions to the celebration of a common humanity. Only by claiming the global as well as the personal dimension of the ecstatic life in the house of love do we truly witness to the presence of Christ, who came to make *all* things new.[153]

In writing about Henri Nouwen in Beth Porter's *Befriending Life*, Jean Vanier observes that 'Henri was truly a gentle instrument of a very loving, tender, and compassionate God.'[154] 'But what an incredible instrument of God!'[155]

Vanier continues, 'Henri became a public spokesman for the mystery at the heart of L'Arche.'[156] Nouwen's teaching, both in person and through his writing, enabled L'Arche to be better known in North America. His bridge-building with other places of worship, in particular his celebration of Sunday Mass in the local parish, made Daybreak's work famous in Richmond Hill. His retreats for leaders of various denominations made Daybreak visible in the Toronto area. Faith and Light support groups for people with disabilities, their families, and volunteers, sprung up, enabled by Nouwen's gifts.

Vanier's understanding of Nouwen was deep and honest: In his eulogy delivered at Nouwen's funeral, Jean talks specifically about Henri, solidarity, compassion, and ecumenism:

> [Nouwen] announced something very important: that unity in our Churches will spring from the poor ... Many will weep at his leaving because he was a sign of hope, a sign of meaning in a divided world with divided Christians.
>   Many people will weep because there was something prophetic in Henri. He accepted pain, he chose to walk through pain because it is the road of all of us. To choose the cross, to walk through the cross, because never will we discover resurrection unless we walk through the cross, unless somewhere we are stripped.[157]

If L'Arche were to mature, these developments could not take place in a vacuum. Nouwen had come to realise this as he writes in his *In the Name of Jesus*:

> Let me tell you about another experience that came out of my move from Harvard to L'Arche. It was the experience of shared ministry. I was educated in a seminary that made me believe that ministry was essentially an individual affair ... Over the years, I realized that things were not as simple as that, but my basic individualistic approach to ministry did not change.[158]
>   When I went to L'Arche, however, this individualism was radically challenged. There I was one of many people who tried to live faithfully with handicapped people, and the fact that I was a priest was not a license to do things on my own.[159]

Individualism was prevalent throughout the church. Nouwen comments: 'When you look at today's Church, it is easy to see the prevalence of individualism among ministers and priests.'[160] And he realises that life in L'Arche enables his priestly ministry to be both communal and mutual, and of a servant leader type: 'I, personally, have been fortunate in having found such a place in L'Arche, with a group of friends who pay attention to my own often-hidden pains and keep me faithful to my vocation by their gentle criticisms and loving support. Would that all priests and ministers could have such a safe place for themselves.'[161]

Nouwen realises, too, the vital importance of being led and guided by others. 'Let me summarize,' he begins. 'My movement from Harvard to L'Arche made me aware in a new way how much my own thinking about Christian leadership had been affected by the desire to be relevant, the desire for popularity, and the desire for power. Too often I looked at being relevant, popular, and powerful as ingredients of an effective ministry,' desires that are all too human. Then, Nouwen argues, 'The truth, however, is that these are not vocations but temptations. Jesus asks, 'Do you love me?' Jesus sends us out to be shepherds, and Jesus promises a life in which we increasingly have to stretch out our hands and be led to places where we do not want to go.' In the letting go of their desires, their vocations, their temptations, a person discovers where they are being led, who is leading, and whom they find: 'He asks us to move from a concern for relevance to a life of prayer, from worries about popularity to communal and mutual ministry, and from a leadership built on power to a leadership in which we critically discern where God is leading us and our people.'[162]

In one of his last books – *Can You Drink the Cup?* – Nouwen sums up his feelings on the true nature of priesthood. 'I have never experienced so deeply that the true nature of priesthood is a compassionate-being-with,' he writes. 'Jesus' priesthood is described in the letter to the Hebrews as one of solidarity with human suffering. Calling myself a priest today radically challenges me to let go of every distance, every little pedestal, every ivory tower, and just to connect my own vulnerability with the vulnerability of those I live with.' And this *kenosis* gives rise to very positive feelings in him: 'And what a joy that is! The joy of belonging, of being part of, of not being different.'[163]

It is not only priests, or professed religious, or missionaries that Nouwen sees as 'Christs' but 'ordinary' people, those who cannot claim any special accomplishments, good deeds, or even the possession of a strong faith, who are living Christs and this fact had its planting in Boisen,[164] its gestation throughout Nouwen's life, and its fruition in L'Arche.

Chapter 4

The Return of the Prodigal Son, the human expression of divine compassion

There have been few spiritual teachers as interested in art as Henri Nouwen was. Art for him was 'a vehicle of prayer that often had a profound and transforming effect on his life and spirituality.'[1] Vincent was like a soul mate. Nouwen also admired Cézanne[2] and knew the work of Chagall.[3] However, the greatest insights were triggered by none of these artists but by another Dutchman, Rembrandt van Rijn (1606-69). Rembrandt's *Prodigal Son*, based on the parable written in Luke 15, changed Nouwen's life and, within it, compassion reached its climax.

Nouwen's stay with Vanier, from November to December 1983, at L'Arche in Trosly-Breuil, was to prove a turning point in the former's spiritual journey that was to be realised more fully later.[4] During Nouwen's visit to Trosly he visited his friend, Simone Landrien, in the community's small documentation centre. As they spoke, Nouwen's eyes fell on a large poster pinned on her office door. On asking Simone to tell him about the poster, she replied 'Oh, that's a reproduction of Rembrandt's *Prodigal Son*. Do you like it?' Nouwen kept staring at the poster and finally professed, 'It's beautiful, more than beautiful ... it makes me want to cry and laugh at the same time ... I can't tell you what I feel as I look at it, but it touches me deeply.' Simone told him, 'Maybe you should have your own copy. You can buy it in Paris.' 'Yes', Nouwen said, 'I must have a copy.'[5] The influence of Rembrandt's work on Nouwen had started.

'The spiritual truth is completely enfleshed'
Just before Nouwen left Trosly-Breuil in July 1986, he was invited by his friends Bobby Massie and his wife, Dana Robert, to join them on a trip to the Soviet Union. Nouwen was thrilled with the idea of seeing the huge

painting – eight feet high by six feet wide – in the Hermitage in Saint Petersburg. Altogether, Nouwen spent over four hours with the *Prodigal Son* and these hours were to bear much fruit. It seems that Rembrandt, Nouwen's 'companion and guide', had made Nouwen aware that his new home was, in fact, to be L'Arche:

> From the moment of my departure, I knew that my decision to join L'Arche on a permanent basis and my visit to the Soviet Union were closely linked. The link – I was sure – was Rembrandt's *Prodigal Son*. Somehow, I sensed that seeing this painting would allow me to enter into the mystery of homecoming in a way I never had before.[6]

While Nouwen was sitting in front of Rembrandt's *Prodigal Son* in the Hermitage in St Petersburg, many tourists passed by. Nouwen records that almost all of the guards described the painting to the tourists as a depiction of the compassionate father. 'Indeed', writes Nouwen, 'this is what this painting is all about. It is the human expression of divine compassion.'[7] Nouwen continues, 'Instead of its being called *The Return of the Prodigal Son*, it could easily have been called "The Welcome by the Compassionate Father."' Certainly, the emphasis is more on the father than on the son and is, in fact, as Nouwen has described, 'a "Parable of the Father's Love."'

> Looking at the way in which Rembrandt portrays the father, there came to me a whole new interior understanding of tenderness, mercy, and forgiveness. Seldom, if ever, has God's immense, compassionate love been expressed in such a poignant way. Every detail of the father's figure – his facial expression, his posture, the colours of his dress, and, most of all, the still gesture of his hands – speaks of the divine love for humanity that existed from the beginning and ever will be.[8]

It was a remarkable epiphany moment. If the Father, that is God the Father, is compassionate, Nouwen realised, then Christians, too, ought to be compassionate. Jesus leaves us in no doubt about this: 'Be compassionate', he commands, 'just as your Father is compassionate' (Lk 6: 36).

God as the Father of Jesus is 'the rock on which his compassionate ministry will be built.'[9] Jesus, the Son of God, is 'The incarnation of divine love ... the expression of God's infinite compassion ... the visible manifestation of the Father's holiness ... the perfect Icon of God.'[10] Nouwen earlier reflected in his *Behold the Beauty of the Lord* (written a few years after *Compassion*, during his retreats to Trosly-Breuil between 1983 and 1986), 'Jesus is the full revelation of God, the image of the unseen God (Col. 1:15). [Jesus' eyes] are the eyes of the one who is "Light from Light, true God from true God, begotten, not made, one in being with the Father ... through whom all things were made" (Nicene Creed). He is indeed the light in whom all is created ... The one who sees unceasingly the limitless goodness of God came to the world, saw it broken to pieces by human sin, and was moved by compassion. The same eyes which see into the heart of God saw the suffering hearts of God's people and wept (see John 11:36).'[11] This is the natural continuation of the *mysterium passionis* about which Nouwen spoke to John Garvey, a priest in the Antiochian Orthodox Church and a long-time friend of Nouwen, in the early 1980s: 'compassion in the most profound sense, is suffering with God; it is an entering into the passion of God.'[12] It is a development of all that Nouwen had discovered in Van Gogh and it is a spiritual insight that people from all traditions within the Christian faith – and beyond – can relate to and benefit from.

> I also see ... infinite compassion, unconditional love, everlasting forgiveness – divine realities – emanating from a Father who is the creator of the universe. Here, both the human and the divine, the fragile and the powerful, the old and the eternally young are fully expressed. This is Rembrandt's genius. The spiritual truth is completely enfleshed.[13]

Reflecting on Philippians 2:7-9, Nouwen comments in *The Genesee Diary* that it was 'only through ultimate sameness', between God the Father and God the Son, that 'Jesus [was] given his unique name.'[14] This is not to play down different gifts, however. The differences across religious and cultural boundaries are manifold, as are the differences between historical divides. What is important is to perceive these differences for what they really are and grow in awareness of what is held in common. A gradual 'attunement of opposite tensions'.[15] In *Out of Solitude* Nouwen also gives this sense of difference as a reason for not responding compassionately to those needing compassion:

> Maybe simply because we ourselves are so concerned to be different from the others that we do not even allow ourselves to lay down our heavy armour and come together in a mutual vulnerability. Maybe we are so full of our own opinions, ideas and convictions that we have no space left to listen to the other and learn from him or her.[16]

At the outset of Chapter 5 the writers of *Compassion* state that the word *ekklesia*, Greek for church, signifies that, as a Christian community, Christians are called (*kaleo* = I call) out (*ek* = out) of their familiar places into the unknown, where people hurt and where they can, with their common human brokenness, experience their common need for healing. It was here, in

Nouwen's own pastoral ministry, undergirded with lessons learnt from both spirituality and psychology, that he was enabled to develop his ecumenical understanding of God's purposes.

'The call to community as we hear it from our Lord is the call to move away from the ordinary and proper places. Leave your father and mother. Let the dead bury the dead. Keep your hand on the plow and do not look back. Sell what you own, give the money to the poor and come follow me' (Lk 14:26; 9:60, 62; 18:22). 'Voluntary displacement leads us to the existential recognition of our inner brokenness and thus brings us to a deeper solidarity with the brokenness of our fellow human beings.'[17] Moreover, 'Voluntary displacement is part of the life of each Christian. It leads away from the ordinary and proper places, whether this is noticed by others or not; it leads to a recognition of each other as fellow travellers on the road, and thus creates community. Finally, voluntary displacement leads to compassion; by bringing us closer to our own brokenness it opens our eyes to our fellow human beings, who seek our consolation and comfort.'[18]

The corollary of this, the three authors argue, is that each and every time Christians desire to move back, to return, to what is ordinary and proper, to be settled and 'feel at home', they build walls between themselves and others, undermine community, and reduce compassion, once again, to the soft part of an essentially competitive life.

St Paul writes that Jesus voluntarily displaced himself: 'His state was divine, yet he did not cling to his equality with God but emptied himself to assume the condition of a slave, and became as we are' (Ph 2:6-7). He became displaced, the three writers continue, so that nothing human – our own displacement – would be alien to him and, moreover, the shared brokenness of our human condition could be fully experienced by him. We see how this displacement continued throughout Jesus' life. He is taken to Egypt to be protected against Herod's threats. He leaves his parents and stays in the Temple, asking questions of, and listening to, the answers of the doctors. He goes to the desert for forty days to fast and be tempted. During his years of ministry we find – or rather lose – him moving away from popularity, power, and success. Ultimately, on earth, he feels abandoned by his heavenly father. 'Jesus' displacement, which began with his birth in Bethlehem, finds its fullest expression in his death on a cross outside the walls of Jerusalem.'[19] His call to voluntary displacement was a call to solidarity with the millions who live disrupted lives.

The paradox of voluntary displacement, Nouwen and his co-authors notice, is that, once undertaken, it places us into a deeper union with the world. Moving from positions of distinction we discover ourselves in positions of sameness, moving from special places, we discover ourselves everywhere.

Benedict's journey to Subiaco, Francis's to the Carceri, Ignatius of Loyola's to Manresa, de Foucauld's to the Sahara, John Wesley's to the poor districts in England, Mother Teresa's to Calcutta and Dorothy Day's to the Bowery are all cited as instances of voluntary displacement. For Merton it meant leaving his teaching position and entering a Trappist monastery. For Luther it meant leaving the monastery and speaking out against scandalous clerical practices. For Bonhoeffer it meant leaving the United States and becoming a prisoner of the Nazis. For Weil it meant leaving her middle class milieu and working in factories. For King it meant leaving the 'ordinary and proper' place for black people and leading protest marches. 'As long as our primary concern in life is to be interesting and thus worthy of special attention, compassion cannot manifest itself. Therefore, the movement toward compassion always starts by gaining distance from the world that wants to make us objects of interest.'[20]

After an exposition of the displacement of Francis of Assisi (1181/1182–1226) – which the authors of *Compassion* regard as 'the most inspiring and challenging example of displacement'[21] – a caveat is delivered: saints and outstanding Christians should never be perceived as people whose behaviour must be imitated. Rather, from their very authenticity and originality, it ought to be perceived that God calls each human being in a unique way and each one ought to be attentive to God's voice in their own unique lives. The warning is earthed by a reminder that whilst we might be dreaming of great acts of displacement, we might fail to notice in the displacements of our own lives the initial indications of God's presence and calling. Voluntary displacement, then, is not primarily something to do or accomplish, but, rather, something to recognise. If we desire to follow our Lord, the three writers argue, we must, primarily, discover in our everyday lives God's unique invitation for each one of us. Although our vocation might not be the same as it was for Dom Helder Camara, Cesar Chavez, Archbishop Romero,[22] or Jean Vanier, each of us is called in as unique a way as to what, when, and where God is calling us.

'I have been led to an inner place where I had not been before. It is the place within me where God has chosen to dwell'

During the year 1985-86, while he was at Trosly-Breuil, Nouwen reflected:

> During that year of transition, I felt especially close to Rembrandt and his *Prodigal Son*. After all, I was looking for a new home. It seemed as though my fellow Dutchman had been given to me as a special companion.[23]

The painting continued to impact on Nouwen. In *The Return of the Prodigal Son*, he records:

> The yearning for a lasting home, brought to consciousness by
> Rembrandt's painting, grew deeper and stronger, somehow making the
> painter himself into a faithful companion and guide.[24]

In 1988, while Nouwen was at Daybreak, he wrote what was arguably to
be one of the finest books he ever wrote, and certainly his most popular
work, *The Return of the Prodigal Son*, based on Rembrandt's painting, to be
published four years later.[25] In July of the same year Nouwen wrote in a letter
to Ed Wojcicki, a friend of his, 'It is a very important book for me and I feel
that I put myself more into that book than any other ... I am very proud of
this book and I hope it can connect me in a good way with many people in
their journeys.'[26]

A decade earlier, just before he began his study of Vincent van Gogh, the
other Dutch artist who made a lasting impression on him, Nouwen had the
idea for *Reaching Out: The Three Movements of the Spiritual Life*, after a 'short,
lively'[27] seminar on Christian spirituality at Yale. *Reaching Out* was finished,
two and a half years later, during a long, quiet sabbatical at the Trappist
Abbey of the Genesee.[28] In it Nouwen explores the three relationships that
became foundational for much of his life work: the relationship to self, to
God, and to others, making evident the impact that Nouwen's studies in
pastoral psychology had had on his ecumenical ministry. The spiritual life
was one that was to be centred in Jesus, reached into oneself, the innermost
being, and to fellow human beings.

The book was like a breath of fresh air. For so many, cut off from the very
ground of their being (which is also 'the ground of all being'[29]), Nouwen
perceives the cause of so much isolation and, at times, alienation, stemming
from the sense of being cut off from all others – who are similarly isolated
– from the natural world (which is being abused and misused), and from
God. Nouwen described three movements: from loneliness – 'one of the most
universal sources of human suffering today'[30] – to solitude (inviting silence)
from hostility to hospitality (inviting ministry), and from life's illusion
to the prayer of the heart (inviting contemplative prayer and community
discernment).[31] And he returns to the same idea twenty years later in *The
Return of the Prodigal Son*,[32] in which the movements are from dissipation to
homecoming, from resentment to gratitude, and from forgiven to forgiver.
Nouwen returns to this concept of movement in the spiritual life a second
time in *Here and Now*,[33] where the movements journeyed from fatalism to
faith, from worrying to prayer, and from mind to heart.

Nouwen considers the idea of spiritual movements in his Prologue from
The Return of the Prodigal Son headed, 'Encounter with a Painting.' Having
described his 'encounters' with both the poster reproduction and the actual

painting of Rembrandt's *Prodigal Son*, Nouwen recalls his early years at
L'Arche Daybreak. He then ends the Prologue with a section titled, 'The
Vision'. In it he considers:

> Rembrandt's painting has remained very close to me throughout this
> time. I moved it around many times: from my office to the chapel, from
> the chapel to the living room of the Dayspring ... and from the living
> room of the Dayspring back to the chapel ... the painting has become
> a mysterious window through which I can step into the Kingdom of
> God. It is like a huge gate that allows me to move to the other side of
> existence and look from there back into the odd assortment of people
> and events that make up my daily life.[34]

Nouwen professes that he has tried 'to get a glimpse of God by looking
carefully at the varieties of human experience,'[35] but then confesses that
'during my time here at Daybreak, I have been led to an inner place where
I had not been before. It is the place within me where God has chosen to
dwell.'[36] A few lines later Nouwen admits, 'This place had always been there I
had always been aware of it as the source of grace.'[37] After much displacement,
self-emptying, and downward growth, Nouwen realises that 'I am called to
enter into the inner sanctuary of my own being where God has chosen to
dwell.'[38] He ends his Prologue with these words:

> The only way to that place is prayer, unceasing prayer. Many struggles
> and much pain can clear the way, but I am certain that only unceasing
> prayer can let me enter it.[39]

From this viewpoint Nouwen is called to 'see' 'an authentically Christian
vision of the world,' as he puts it, 'looking at people and this world through
the eyes of God.'[40] From this vantage point he is able to speak and write into
his own and others' lives. Listening to 'the heartbeat of God,'[41] he can say
what he hears. He is, he writes, 'well aware of the enormity of this vocation,'
but is 'confident that it is the only way for me.'[42]

In one of his earliest books, *With Open Hands*, published in 1972 and
revised in 1995, Nouwen, in a passage on compassion rare for that period,
explains that compassion is to be rooted in prayer, because compassion must
be rooted in trust in God:

> Compassion is possible when it has its roots in prayer. For in prayer you
> are not based on your own strength, not on the good will of another, but
> only on trust in God. That is why prayer is primarily a calling to find
> your own place in this world and to live in that place. There it is that

you not only discover that you exist, but you meet people next to you, who with you will cultivate and develop the new world.[43]

The concept of rooting compassion in prayer is returned to in *Here and Now* (1994). Here, Nouwen writes, 'When I pray, I enter into the depth of my own heart and find there the heart of God, who speaks to me of love. And I recognize, right there, the place where all of my sisters and brothers are in communion with one another.'[44]

In another book from the early 1970s, *The Genesee Diary* (written in 1974), Nouwen explains:

> Often I have said to people, 'I will pray for you,' but how often did I really enter into the full reality of what that means? I now see how indeed I can enter deeply into the other and pray to God from his center. When I really bring my friends and the many I pray for into my innermost being and feel their pains, their struggles, their cries in my own soul, then I leave myself, so to speak, and become them, then I have compassion. Compassion lies at the heart of our prayer for our fellow human beings. When I pray for the world, I become the world; when I pray for the endless needs of the millions, my soul expands and wants to embrace them all and bring them into the presence of God. But in the midst of that experience I realize that compassion is not mine but God's gift to me. I cannot embrace the world, but God can. I cannot pray, but God can pray in me. When God became as we are, that is, when God allowed all of us to enter into his intimate life, it became possible for us to share in his infinite compassion.
>
> In praying for others, I lose myself and become the other, only to be found by the divine love which holds the whole of humanity in a compassionate embrace.[45]

Developing out of the writing in *With Open Hands*, Nouwen argues in *Out of Solitude*, a book that was to be published only two years later in 1974, that compassion is required of all who live in relationship with God.[46] Yet many Christians, he remarks, have little or no space left in their lives to listen to those needing compassion, or to allow them to draw near, because of their own busy-ness.

Bombarded by so much attention in the media on the pains and sufferings in the world, 'our continued effectiveness requires a mental filtering system by which we can moderate the impact of the daily news.' Moreover, 'exposure to human misery on a mass scale can lead not only to psychic numbness but also to hostility.'[47] As such, 'The Christian community mediates between the suffering of the world and our individual responses to this suffering ...

it enables us to be fully aware of the painful condition of the human family without being paralyzed by this awareness.'[48] 'In community, we are ... transformed into one people of God. In community ... we become gentle manifestations of God's boundless compassion. In community, our lives become compassionate ... By our life together, we become participants in the divine compassion.' Further, 'since it is in community that God's compassion reveals itself, solidarity, servanthood, and obedience are also the main characteristics of our life together.'[49]

Nouwen and his co-authors close the fourth chapter of *Compassion* with words that witness to his insights gained from both psychology and theology:

> Without a sense of being sent by a caring community, a compassionate life cannot last long and quickly degenerates into a life marked by numbness and anger. This is not simply a psychological observation, but a theological truth, because apart from a vital relationship with a caring community a vital relationship with Christ is not possible.[50]

'A place of surrender and complete trust'

> It is the place where I receive all that I desire, all that I ever hoped for, all that I will ever need, but it is also the place where I have to let go of all that I most want to hold onto. It is the place that confronts me with the fact that truly accepting love, forgiveness, and healing is often much harder than giving it. It is the place beyond earning, deserving and rewarding. It is a place of surrender and complete trust.[51]

Few sentences better encapsulate Nouwen's feelings of intimacy within community. These feelings, expressed in the opening pages of *The Return of the Prodigal Son*, had nourished a compassionate approach to Christian living which he had been experiencing at L'Arche. Over his years at Daybreak, Rembrandt's painting continued to exert a lasting impression on Nouwen. It was almost as if the painting worked in Nouwen as 'a powerful instrument of grace'.[52]

Compassion is not, cannot be by virtue of its very nature, an individualistic trait of character. It is, essentially, a way of living together. Paul, *inter alia*, emphasises the fact that the compassionate life is life in community: 'If our life in Christ means anything to you, if love can persuade at all, or the Spirit that we have in common, or any tenderness and sympathy, then be united in your convictions and united in your love, with a common purpose and a common mind' (Phil 2:1-2).

It is by the way in which Christians live and work together that they witness to God's compassionate presence. The first converts 'revealed their conversion

not by feats of individual stardom but by entering a new life in community'
(see Acts 2:44-47). 'A compassionate life', the co-writers of *Compassion* write,
'is a life in which ... we enter into a new relationship with each other ...
[in which] fellowship with Christ reveals itself in a new fellowship among
those who follow him ... Compassion, then, can never be separated from
community. Compassion always reveals itself in community, in a new way
of being together ... the body of Christ ... [where Jesus Christ] ... is present
as the compassionate Lord.'[53]

It is important to emphasise here the fact that Nouwen's empathy with
Rembrandt was made most manifest during the former's darkest months.
Nouwen became obsessed with the painting. During Nouwen's breakdown,
books on the life and work of Rembrandt were to provide solace. During
those bleak months, along with Nouwen's reading of Van Gogh's letters and
looking at reproductions of Van Gogh's art work, he derived great consolation
from studying the life of the Dutch artist whose own journey had ultimately
enabled him to paint the masterpiece. It was a journey that had witnessed
great tragedy, which affected Nouwen profoundly. Rembrandt's wife, Saskia,
died at an early age, leaving the artist to care for his nine-month-old son,
Titus, who survived childhood and adolescence. Another son, Rumbartus,
died in 1635 at the age of six. Rembrandt also lost two daughters, Cornelia
in 1638 and a second daughter also named Cornelia in 1640. After Saskia
died, Rembrandt became involved in several unsuccessful relationships. His
financial worries worsened, resulting in the sale of his possessions in auctions.
Even the happiness experienced with the marriage of his son Titus was short-
lived. Titus died within a year of marrying. 'One must have died many deaths
and cried many tears to have painted a portrait of God in such humility,'
Nouwen proclaims in his *The Return of the Prodigal Son*.

> The few books I could take with me were all about Rembrandt and
> the parable of the prodigal son. While living in a rather isolated place,
> far away from my friends and community, I found great consolation
> in reading the tormented life of the great Dutch painter and learning
> more about the agonizing journey that ultimately had enabled him to
> paint this magnificent work.
>
> For hours I looked at the splendid drawings and paintings he created
> in the midst of all his setbacks, disillusionment, and grief, and I came
> to understand how from his brush there emerged the figure of a nearly
> blind old man holding his son in a gesture of all-forgiving compassion.[54]

Nowhere does Nouwen himself describe more clearly what resting in God
meant for him than in a passage from *The Return of the Prodigal Son*.[55]

'Coming home' meant, for Nouwen, returning from an exhausting lecture tour to Trosly-Breuil, which he fascinatingly describes as 'a safe place'.[56] It also meant leaving the world of teachers and students to live in L'Arche. And it meant meeting the people of a country – Russia – that had separated itself from the rest of the world by walls and heavily guarded borders. But, above all, 'coming home' meant 'walking step by step toward the One who awaits me with open arms and wants to hold me in an eternal embrace.'[57] Trosly-Breuil and L'Arche were to be 'home' for Nouwen for the final decade or so of his life. Russia, or more specifically Saint Petersburg, was to enable Nouwen to connect with men and women who had been cut off from the rest of humankind. But the ultimate homecoming was, of course, to return gradually to God who had been patiently waiting to embrace Nouwen not just for the remainder of his earthly life but for the whole of eternity. And it was Rembrandt who, through his *Prodigal Son*, was to express this resting in God most clearly and influence Nouwen most penetratingly in reflecting what this resting meant. Nouwen knew that Rembrandt deeply understood this spiritual homecoming.

> I knew that, when Rembrandt painted his *Prodigal Son*, he had lived a life that had left him with no doubt about his true and final home.[58]

In fact, it was soon after completing his *Prodigal Son* that Rembrandt died. Nouwen felt that, if he could meet Rembrandt 'right where he had painted father and son, God and humanity, compassion and misery, in one circle of love,'[59] he would come to know as much as he ever would about life and death. 'I also sensed the hope that through Rembrandt's masterpiece I would one day be able to express what I most wanted to say about love.'[60]Having reflected on the *Prodigal Son*, Nouwen was enabled to write about that love that finds its rest in God which is there for all people, irrespective of whether or not they are Christian, whether or not they know about Christ, whether or not they are aware of the Holy Spirit working in their lives.

'It is the human expression of divine compassion'

Nouwen sums up the meaning of Rembrandt's *Prodigal Son* in one sentence: 'It is the human expression of divine compassion.' As such, Rembrandt depicts elements of solidarity, consolation, and comfort. There is solidarity in the standing alongside of the father, his two sons, and his servants, and also in the viewer looking at the painting, consolation in the immense sense of peace that the painting both manifests in the father's everlasting embrace and the younger son's eternal rediscovery of his deepest self as he rests against his father's breast,[61] and evokes in the viewer,[62] and comfort in the returning home, and in the heart and mind of the viewer, too, whose attention is drawn to the warm hues of the father's cloak and the relaxed yet firm position of his hands, drawing his younger son to himself.

God the Father has come to humankind in Jesus. Reflecting on Matthew 3:16-17, Nouwen goes on to write in *Here and Now*, 'Jesus speaks and lives as the Beloved Son of God.'[63] In his meditations on the parable of the prodigal son, too, Nouwen had written that all that Jesus says concerning himself reveals him as the Beloved Son, 'the one who lives in complete communion with the Father.'[64] There is no separation between Father and Son. There is no division of work, no competition, no envy. There is perfect unity between them. Further, as Nouwen had written, again two years earlier in 1990, 'In and through Jesus, our world can become one because in his divine love he embraces all of us and desires that we all will be one as he and his Father are one (see John 17:21).'[65]

Meditating on the parable of the prodigal son in the early 1990s, Nouwen came to realise, 'Perhaps the most radical statement that Jesus ever made is: "Be compassionate as your Father is compassionate." God's compassion is described by Jesus not simply to show me how willing God is to feel for me, or to forgive me my sins and offer me new life and happiness, but to invite me to become like God and to show the same compassion to others as he is showing to me.' Nouwen adds, in one of the most radical statements that *he* makes: 'If the only meaning of the story were that people sin but God forgives, I could easily begin to think of my sins as a fine occasion for God to show me his forgiveness. There would be no real challenge in such an interpretation ... Such sentimental romanticism is not the message of the Gospels ... As son and heir I am to become successor. I am destined to step into my Father's place and offer to others the same compassion that he has offered me. The return to the Father is ultimately the challenge to become the Father.'[66]

In 1992, that is a decade after the publication of *Compassion*, Nouwen in *The Return of the Prodigal Son*, uses the metaphor of the prodigal son's father to illustrate the concept that Christians are to become like the Father, to be 'compassionate as your heavenly Father is compassionate,' to offer the same compassion that he has offered them and to become transformed into his image. In Rembrandt's depiction of the father, and his two sons, compassion, inter-personal relationship, and unity are captured and made visible.

This dispels any idea of the compassionate life as 'a life of heroic self-denial'. 'Compassion, as a downward movement towards solidarity instead of an upward movement towards popularity, does not require heroic gestures or a sensational turn-around.'[67] In actual fact, the compassionate life is hidden within the ordinariness of everyday living: to be there, alongside the insecure teenager, the estranged husband and wife, the isolated gay person, the lonely pensioner. 'Once we look downward instead of upward on the ladder of life, we see the pain of people wherever we go, and we hear the call of compassion wherever we are. True compassion always begins right where we are.'[68]

Nouwen had known, in theory, the truth and authenticity of what he had been teaching throughout his adult life. Now, at L'Arche Daybreak, he experiences this truth and authenticity with his heart. He confesses: 'The painting has become a mysterious window through which I can step into the Kingdom of God.'[69] 'But I had not been able to enter it and truly live there.'[70] He admits, 'I was not as familiar with the home of God within me as I am now.'[71] Nouwen questions, 'Had I, myself, really ever dared to step into the center, kneel down, and let myself be held by a forgiving God?'[72] No, he hadn't, and, knowing that there had been periods in his life when he had not prayed, he writes, 'I am certain that only unceasing prayer can let me enter it.'[73] Nouwen admits, 'These years at Daybreak have not been easy.'[74] 'The journey from teaching about love to allowing myself to be loved proved much longer than I realized.'[75] The grain of wheat had fallen and, now, much fruit was indeed to be produced. Broken open by his breakdown, Nouwen was now able to apply himself to living compassionately in a way that ecclesiastical institutions were not and could not – through '[making] the connection between prayer and life,'[76] '[witnessing] in a way that [he] never could have [done] before,'[77] and '[recognising] the presence of Jesus in a radically new way,'[78] Nouwen enabled everyone to come together on a daily basis in order to have a personal experience of Jesus and, having come closer together, to live out the Gospel imperative to love compassionately.

The penultimate chapter of *Compassion* opens with the words 'The discipline of patience is practiced in prayer and action.'[79] 'Prayer must be our first concern ... Prayer is the discipline by which we liberate the Spirit of God from entanglement in our impatient impulses. It is the way by which we allow God's Spirit to move freely.'[80]

Until Chapter 8 of *Compassion* the Holy Spirit has barely been mentioned but now it is made clear that it is the Holy Spirit who enables people to live with 'a new mind in a new time ... and prayer itself is the expression of the life of the Holy Spirit in us ... as a discipline of patience [prayer] is the human effort to allow the Holy Spirit to do re-creating work in us.'[81] The discipline of prayer, the authors continue, involves the continual choice not to flee, but to listen carefully, not to clutter our minds with distractions, and, above all, to set aside time every day to be alone with God and listen to the Holy Spirit, for the Spirit enables us to come to the awareness of all that Jesus said and did (Jn 14:26, 16:8), to pray (Rm 8:26-27), and to be witnesses (Ac 1:8). Then we may be assured of the truth (Rm 9:1), receive righteousness, peace and joy (Rm 14:17), have all boundaries to hope removed (Rm 15:13), and recognise the newness of everything (Tt 3:5).[82] As such the discipline of prayer is a form of inner displacement, in which the Spirit of the compassionate God is revealed, and discipleship is supported.

Prayer is also the first expression of human solidarity because the Holy Spirit who prays in each person is the same Holy Spirit that brings all human beings together in unity and community. This same Holy Spirit is the power through whom people are brought together as brothers and sisters of the same Christ and sons and daughters of the same God. And in this unity, community, and togetherness the Holy Spirit reveals God as the God who loves all members of the human family and enables a growing intimacy with God that deepens a sense of responsibility for others. 'Prayer is the very beat of a compassionate heart ... making [others] part of ourselves ... so that in and through us they can be touched by the healing power of God's Spirit,'[83]involving friction, risk and struggle, but, ultimately, harmony.

Compassionate prayer for every human being is at the very centre of Christian life. It is a mark of the Christian community (Rm 1: 9; 2 Co 1:11; Ep 6:8; Col 4:3), bringing help and even salvation to all for whom prayer is offered up (Rm 15:30; Ph 1:19). It allows us to bring to the very centre of our heart not only those who love us but also those who hate us. Nouwen quotes Dietrich Bonhoeffer (1906-45) who expresses the concept that there are no boundaries to prayers. Bonhoeffer writes powerfully and simply when he states that to pray for others is to give them 'the same right we have received, namely, to stand before Christ and share in his mercy.'[84]   Yet, when asked to listen and empathise, people can soon reach their emotional limit. People are able to listen only for a while and only to a few. People are being constantly bombarded by so much news involving human misery that they can either become burnt out or numb. God's heart, so full of compassion, is without limit. It neither burns out nor does it become numb.

> It is for this compassionate heart that we pray when we pray: 'A pure heart create for me, O God, put a steadfast spirit within me. Do not cast me away from your presence, nor deprive me of your holy spirit.' (Ps 51:11-12)[85]

In receiving this pure heart that loves compassionately, in receiving the Holy Spirit who enables compassion, in constantly depending on God, each person can become a little more Christ-like. Indeed, Nouwen concludes his chapter on compassion in *Here and Now* with the words, 'The Holy Spirit of God is given us so that we can become participants in God's compassion and so reach out to all people at all times with God's heart.'[86] Here we enter into the relationship argued by Athanasius of Alexandria (*c.* 297–373), the relationship in which Christ became man in order that we might become

God. The Father, in making himself visible in Jesus' body, enabled us to have an idea of the invisible Father.[87]

Some years later, Nouwen was to make explicit the significance of the painting, through which the work of retrieval continued:

> It has now been more than six years since I first saw the Rembrandt poster at Trosly and five years since I decided to make L'Arche my home. As I reflect on these years, I realize that the people with a mental handicap and their assistants make me 'live' Rembrandt's painting more completely than I could have anticipated. The warm welcomes I have received in many L'Arche houses and the many celebrations I have shared have allowed me to experience deeply the younger son's return. Welcome and celebration are, indeed, two of the main characteristics of life 'in the Ark'. There are so many welcome signs, hugs and kisses, songs, skits, and festive meals that for an outsider L'Arche may appear a lifelong homecoming celebration.[88]

Nouwen's stepping into the centre, his kneeling down, and allowing himself to be held, mirroring the Prodigal Son before his forgiving father, had taken place in its earthly fullness at L'Arche. Nouwen had heard God's call and had responded. God had continued to hold Nouwen, too, during the months of his breakdown. Obedience to that call had issued in overwhelming blessings and it was an aspect of compassion that Nouwen and his co-authors had explored in *Compassion*.

The God of compassion, they had written, is not only a God who serves but also a God who serves *in obedience*.[89] Nouwen and his two co-writers state, 'God's compassion is not made manifest simply by becoming a suffering servant, but by becoming a suffering servant in obedience.' 'Obedience', they add, 'gives servanthood its deepest dimension.'

Here is another challenge. There can be an insidious side to serving one's fellow human beings, giving one's time to the poor, and living in solidarity with those who suffer. We can decide what to do and when to do it. We can control our servanthood. Nevertheless, there can be a subtle element of manipulation in our serving. As long as we can become our own masters again, as long as we can determine when to begin and end our serving, where we can serve, and to whom, can we really say that we are servants?

In Jesus' self-emptying, compassion is perceived not only as servanthood but also as obedience. The Roman Catholic writers of *Compassion* quote the Protestant Barth a second time: 'It belongs to the inner life of God that there should take place within it obedience ... in himself he is both One who is obeyed and Another who obeys.'[90] 'Through Jesus' complete obedience

God compassionately entered into our broken, wounded, and painful human condition.'[91] The word obedience is derived from the Latin verb *audire*, which means 'to listen.' Obedience, then, as embodied in Christ, is 'a total listening, a giving attention with no hesitation or limitation ... it is an expression of the intimacy that can exist between two persons ... the expression of his most intimate, loving relationship.'[92] In Jesus' obedient servanthood, therefore, is perceived 'a divine listening to a divine love, a loving response to a loving mission, and a free "yes" to a free command.'[93] Jesus' first words spoken in the Temple were, 'Did you not know that I must be busy with my Father's affairs' (Lk 2:49). His last words on the cross, 'Father, into your hands I commit my spirit' (Lk 23:46). Here is a life solely dedicated to carrying out the will of God. Jesus' ministry was one of obedient listening, obedient servanthood. As Jesus himself professes, 'I can do nothing by myself ... my aim is to do not my own will, but the will of him who sent me' (Jn 5:30). As Paul remarks, 'He humbled himself and became obedient unto death' (Ph 2:8). Again, an obedience that did not seek out pain and suffering but to give its undivided attention to the voice of his Father.

Moreover, Jesus did not enter the world, clinging to his intimate relationship with the Father, but to include everyone in his divine obedience, to lead everyone to God, in order that all may share in this divine intimacy. All are called to be sons and daughters of God, brothers and sisters of one another, to listen, to be obedient, and to be enabled to be no less compassionate than Jesus himself.

God is a compassionate God. That is the good news brought in and through Jesus Christ, God-with-us, who finds nothing human alien and who lives in solidarity with all. Jesus is a servant God who washes our feet and heals our wounds, an obedient God who listens and responds with unlimited love. In companionship with Jesus Christ, all are called to be compassionate as our loving God is compassionate. In and through him, it becomes possible to be effective witnesses to God's compassion and to be signs of hope in the midst of a despairing world.[94]

Christians are further challenged not simply to live compassionate lives but to show that this compassion points beyond the here and now. In the Conclusion to *Compassion* McNeill, Morrison, and Nouwen refer to the Book of Revelation. Here the vision of a new heaven and a new earth is offered:

> And I heard a loud voice call from the throne, saying, 'See, the home of God is among mortals. He will dwell with them; they will be his peoples, and God ... will be with them; he will wipe every tear from their eyes. Death will be no more; mourning and crying will be no more; for the first things have passed away.' (Rv 21:3-4)

The vision adds a greater depth to our way of living the new life. Already we are sharing one another's burdens, carrying each other's crosses, and being guided together towards a new way of life. We are welcoming the stranger, clothing the naked, visiting the prisoners and the sick, and overcoming oppression. Through these actions we glimpse something of what is meant by 'a new heaven and a new earth'. God will live with us and already each time two or three gather Jesus is among us. All tears will be wiped away and already each time people share bread and wine in Jesus' memory, smiles appear on tear-stained faces. The whole of creation will be renewed and already the old earth is giving way to the new. 'This is the foundation of our faith, the basis of our hope, and the source of our love.'[95]

Compassion does not end with a chapter headed Conclusion. Rather, it ends with an Epilogue accompanied by seven illustrations which, as the co-writers add, 'may prove to be more important than the words.'[96] They are by Joel Filártiga, a medical doctor, who was living with his wife, Nidia, and seventeen-year-old son, Joelito, and working with the poorest of the poor in Paraguay. He had a small clinic in Ybyqui, two hours' drive from the capital city of Asunción. When McNeill, Morrison and Nouwen were reflecting on compassion, it came to their notice that on 30 March 1976 Joelito was murdered by a police squad torturing him by burning and electro-shocks. This above all taught the writers what compassion is. 'It is a willingness to lay down our lives for our friends.'[97] And if these writers' voices were to have any authenticity or authority in the modern world, they would need to champion the voiceless of the South, and, in so doing, would need to 'listen hard and read these signs of the times,'[98] for the Vatican document *Gaudium et spes* recognised the mission of the Church, not just to the West and East, but to diverse people in Africa, Asia, and Latin America as well.[99]

After his sabbatical in 1995-96, Nouwen returned briefly to Daybreak then visited his father in the Netherlands and was preparing to make a return journey to Russia in order to make a film about *The Return of the Prodigal Son* when he suffered two heart attacks. He passed away in Hilversum on Saturday, 21 September 1996, aged sixty-four. 'In the hour of the wolf'[100] he dies alone.[101]

Life [is] a long process of dying to self, so that we will be able to live in the joy of God and give our lives completely to others.[102]

Closing thoughts

After almost completing my thesis, I stumbled across a document of which I had previously been unaware and discovered in an extraordinary way that it corroborated much of what I had already written. The document is a double-sided synopsis of Henri Nouwen's life entitled *My History with God* that Nouwen himself wrote during the autumn of 1994 for a class he was teaching at Regis College, the Jesuit Graduate Faculty of Theology, a member institution of the Toronto School of Theology, within the University of Toronto.[1]

The synopsis is in three uneven parts. The first, an autobiographical summary, falls into three sections: 'The Safe Home' (covering the years 1932-1957); 'Breaking Down All Boundaries' (1957-1986); and 'A New Home' (1986-1994). In the second part Nouwen simply notes that he has been 'deeply influenced by the works and writings of Vincent van Gogh, the art of Rembrandt, and the friendship of some contemporary artists.'[2] The final part states 'The movement that obviously has most affected my life is l'Arche, but also other worlds have affected me. The world of the circus, the world of AIDS ministry, the world of Latin America, and the world of Eastern Europe (especially Ukraine) have all had a significant impact on my life.'[3]

Nouwen writes in *My History with God* that the first 24 years of his life were 'basically years to prepare [him]self for the Catholic priesthood ... It was a time in which all the boundaries were very clear.'[4] The knowledge that he was a Roman Catholic and not a Protestant, that he was a Christian and not a Moslem, Buddhist, or Hindu, that he was a believer and not a pagan, that he was Dutch and not German, French, or English and that he was white and not black gave him 'a sense of being in the right place, being wholly protected, and being very safe.'[5] He did not meet anybody who was divorced, who had left the priesthood, or who was gay.

Nouwen's upbringing and seminary training unequivocally set out what he was going to do as a priest. There were no doubts here. 'I knew the right teaching and the right way to live the moral life' he professes. 'Six years in the seminary had given me very clear-cut guidelines and surrounded me with people who had received the same guidelines. Proclaiming the Gospel and administering the sacraments were challenging, but not complicated, and something I really felt called to do.' He concludes, 'I was a very happy person, felt very close to God, had a very disciplined prayer life and a very clear-cut vocation. I was ordained in July 1957.'[6] Ten years later Nouwen was to meet Merton.

Nouwen himself continues in Part 2 that he was 'deeply influenced' by the works and writings of Vincent van Gogh and the art of Rembrandt. '[They] broke down the several fences that had given me a safe garden, and made me deeply aware that God's covenant with God's people includes everyone.'[7]

It was a journey from the years of *exclusivity*, the years in which, as he describes in his *History*, '[he] lived a life in which [he] related exclusively to Roman Catholics,'[8] to the years of *inclusivity*, the years in which he was enabled to 'know that living with the people of my community [was] calling [him] to be a witness to God in a way that [he] never could have been before.'[9]

'For me personally', writes Nouwen, 'This was a time of searching, questioning and often agonizing. A time that was extremely lonely and not without moments of great inner uncertainty and ambiguity. The Jesus that I had come to know in my youth had died. I was travelling in a downcast way to Emmaus, and started hearing the Voice of someone who had joined me on the journey.'[10] Nevertheless, it was also a fruitful time, and a time of increasing acceptance, both of self and of others: 'During all these years, I learned that Protestants belong as much to the church as Catholics, and that Hindus, Buddhists, and Moslems believe in God as much as Christians do; that pagans can love one another as much as believers can; that human psyche is multidimensional; that theology, psychology, and sociology are intersecting in many places; that women have a real call to ministry; that homosexual people have a unique vocation in the Christian community; that the poor belong to the heart of the church; and that the spirit of God blows where it wants.'[11]

In the third and final part Nouwen adds, 'When I joined the L'Arche Daybreak Community in Toronto, I was searching for a new home. I knew it could not be the old home that I had left, but I did not know what the new home would look like.'[12] Then he makes a profession, declaring how living in this 'New Home' had changed his relationship with Jesus: 'During the last eight years living with people with mental handicaps and their assistants in a very close knit community consisting of people from many different religions, backgrounds, communities, and lifestyles, my heart started to burn, and I started to recognise the presence of Jesus in a radically new way.'[13]

Indeed, this is borne out by Michael O'Laughlin who makes the significant comment in *God's Beloved* that the year 1985, the year in which Nouwen began his extended stay at Trosly-Breuil marked 'the beginning of a turn in Henri's life back to Jesus, one that would continue to renew itself and bear fruit for the rest of his life.'[14]

In *My History with God* Nouwen concludes, 'During this time I have experienced much loneliness, much confusion, and much insecurity, but I have experienced all of this sorrow living with poor people who in their simplicity and openness offer me a space that gradually could become a new home. Since living in community, my spiritual journey has been radically deepened, the full dimension of which I am not yet fully able to articulate.'[15] It was ultimately the openness of the people with learning disabilities and their assistants who, in an ecumenical (and to a certain extent interfaith) community together, showed Nouwen the *significance* of a life that is Christo-centric, deeply personal yet profoundly universal in scope, and, perhaps, may show the ecclesiastical institutions the *significance* of a life that is compassionate, ecumenical and interfaith, not as an *alternative* way forward but as a *means* of moving forward.

Together, Merton, Van Gogh, Vanier and Rembrandt anticipated Nouwen in their retrieval of an authentically Christian vision of the world, a vision in which all people could rest in God, and know and commit themselves to Jesus, through the co-operation of the Holy Spirit: a vision within which compassion could be nurtured. Their intense and unwavering influence on Nouwen was such that he desired and was enabled to retrieve this vision, through resting in God, centring on Jesus, and discerning the gifts of the Spirit as his mentors had done before him. Their collective lives and work, considered here for the first time, have been seen to emerge as a unifying presence and theological wellspring in Nouwen's life and writing. Together, these four pivotal mentors served to catalyse, centre, and nurture Nouwen's outreach to others, particularly in the crucial importance they attached to living compassionate lives, whose significance, until now, has remained understudied.

On 22 June 1996, Nouwen makes the following extraordinary entry in his diary:

> Following the celebration from a great distance, I realized how much I miss the intimate home liturgies at Daybreak ... For some reason, I became sad and melancholy realizing that this was *my* church, *my* spirituality, and *my* liturgy. I felt like an outsider, a tourist, an observer. When we left, I said to my father, 'Tomorrow, we'd better celebrate the Eucharist in my bedroom. That might save ... me a depression.'[16]

Henri had been attending Mass with his father, Laurent, in the very large Trappist monastery at Orval in Villers-devant-Orval, part of Florenville, which is in the province of Luxembourg. Now, Nouwen certainly did not approach the Mass as a typical Roman Catholic priest (if such a being does indeed exist), simply steeped in the inherited tradition of the Roman Catholic part of the Church, but just how far he had in fact journeyed from the earliest days of his ministry, through academia, Genesee, Latin America, and L'Arche is brought home to us in these few lines.

'Life is a long journey of preparation – of preparing oneself to truly die for others ... Life [is] a long process of dying to self, so that we will be able to live in the joy of God and give our lives completely to others.'[17] There is here an awareness of the taking, blessing, breaking, and giving, that Nouwen developed: 'I know now that the words spoken to Jesus when he was baptized are words spoken also to me and to all who are brothers and sisters of Jesus.'[18] And, a couple of pages later: 'I have to belong to God while giving myself to people.'[19] 'When I awoke from my operation ... I had an immediate perception of being sent: sent to make the all-embracing love of the Father known to people who hunger and thirst for love but often look for it within a world where it cannot be found.'[20]

In the closing pages of *Beyond the Mirror*, written as a reflection after his serious brush with death, Nouwen earths what he has been experiencing and writing with his newfound family in L'Arche and, in so doing, returns to the theme of taking, blessing, breaking, and giving:

> They [the core members] are always 'in intensive care,' always dependent, always in the portal of death. They can bring me in touch and hold me close to that place in me where I am like them: weak, broken, and totally dependent. It is the place of true poverty where God calls me blessed and says to me, 'Don't be afraid. You are my beloved child, on whom my favour rests.'[21]

Nouwen writes in his foreword to Gijs Okhuijsen's *In Heaven there are no Thunderstorms: Celebrating the Liturgy with Developmentally Disabled People*, 'Jesus did not say, "Blessed are those who care for the poor," but "Blessed are the poor." We are all poor. It is precisely in our poverty that we need to speak and hear the words of healing.'[22]

Together, Merton, Van Gogh, Vanier and Rembrandt opened up Nouwen's heart to respond compassionately to people, especially the marginalised, to come alongside and connect with an abundant number of friends, and to enter into and offer healing to their vulnerability. At the same time, these four mentors enabled Nouwen to experience more deeply God's own compassion, through resting in the Father, accompanying and being accompanied by Christ in his downward mobility, and perceiving three gifts of the Spirit: solidarity, consolation, and comfort. These were all key theological concepts that were shared in common between Nouwen and his mentors and were to prove of paramount importance for Nouwen's understanding of compassion. This was best seen in the retrieval of nothing less than an authentically Christian vision of the world, attaching crucial importance to living compassionate lives, and responding to the Gospel imperative to love.

Integrated Chronological Bibliography [1]

(The following Chronological Bibliography integrates Henri Nouwen's books with the principal events of his life.)

1932, Sunday, 24 January, Henri Josef Machiel Nouwen born to Laurent and Maria in Nijkerk, the Netherlands

1950-57, trains for the priesthood, first at the minor seminary of Apeldoon where his maternal uncle, Monsignor Anton (Toon) C. Ramselaar, was president, and then at the Roman Catholic Diocesan Seminary in Rijsenburg in the province of Utrecht

1957, 21 July, ordained by Archbishop Bernard Alfrink, Primate of the Netherlands, at St Catherine's Cathedral, Utrecht, to the Roman Catholic priesthood

1957-64, studies psychology at the Catholic University of Nijmegen, the Netherlands, in preference to pursuing his studies in theology at the Gregorian University in Rome

1962-65, in Rome at the time of the Second Vatican Council[2]

1964, visits America as a chaplain aboard the Holland-America Line[3]

1964, meets with Anton T. Boisen

1964-66, Fellow in the programme for Religion and Psychiatry at the Menninger Clinic, Kansas

1966-68, visiting Professor in the Psychology Department at the University of Notre Dame

1966-68,[4] *Intimacy: Pastoral Psychological Essays* published 1969

1966-68, *Creative Ministry: Beyond Professionalism in Teaching, Preaching, Counselling, Organizing and Celebrating* published 1971

1968-70, *Bidden om het Leven, Het Contemplatief engagement van Thomas Merton* published 1970

1967,[5] 7 May, meets Merton at the Abbey of Gethsemani, Kentucky

1968-69, Staff Member at the Joint Pastoral Institute, Amsterdam

1969-70, Faculty Member and Chairman of Department of Behavioural Sciences of the Catholic Theological Institute, Utrecht

1970, *Met Open Handen: Notities over het gebed* published 1971

1970-72, *The Wounded Healer: Ministry in Contemporary Society* published 1972

1970-71, theological studies at the Catholic University of Nijmegen

1971, Autumn, to 1977, Associate Professor of Pastoral Theology at Yale Divinity School

1972, ET of *Bidden om het Leven* by David Schlaver with assistance by Nouwen as *Pray to Live*

1972, ET of *Met Open Handen* by Patrick Gaffney as *With Open Hands*

1974, receives tenure of post at Yale Divinity School

1974, *Out of Solitude: Three Meditations on the Christian Life* published 1974

1974, *Aging: The Fulfillment of Life* co-authored with Walter Gaffney

1974, June-December, stays at the Abbey of the Genesee

1974, *Reaching Out: The Three Movements of the Spiritual Life* published 1975

1974-75, *The Genesee Diary: Report from a Trappist Monastery* published 1976

1975, begins to study the work of Van Gogh and develops an affinity with the artist that lasts for the remainder of his life

1976, Resident Scholar at the Institute for Ecumenical and Cultural Research, Collegeville, Minnesota

1976, *The Living Reminder: Service and Prayer in Memory of Jesus Christ* published 1977

1977-81, Professor of Pastoral Theology at Yale Divinity School

1977, October, receives honorary degree from Yale

1978, Spring, Scholar-in-Residence at the Pontifical North American College in Rome, also lectures at Pontifical Beda College, Rome, and to the Unione Internazionale delle Superiori Generali

1978, *Clowning in Rome: Reflections on Solitude, Celibacy, Prayer, and Contemplation* 1979

1978, Summer, spends several summers with Parker Palmer and leads retreats at Pendle Hill, in Wallingford, Pennsylvania

1978, 9 October, Mother dies

1978, *In Memoriam* published 1980

1979, February to July, stays at the Abbey of the Genesee

1979, *A Cry for Mercy: Prayers from the Genesee* published 1981

1979, *A Letter of Consolation* published 1982

?-1981, *Making All Things New: An Invitation to the Spiritual Life* published 1981

1981, *The Way of the Heart: Desert Spirituality and Contemporary Ministry*

1981, *Compassion: A Reflection on the Christian Life* co-authored with McNeill and Morrison published 1982

1981, July, resigns from Yale Divinity School

1981, Nouwen and Vanier meet for the first time, on a retreat at South Bend, near Chicago

1981-82, Family Brother at the Abbey of the Genesee

1981, October, to March, 1982, stays in Bolivia, Lima and Peru then returns to the Abbey of the Genesee

1981-82, *¡Gracias! A Latin American Journal* published 1983

1983, January, in Mexico to meet with the Center of Economical and Social Studies of the Third World

1983-86, *Lifesigns: Intimacy, Fecundity, and Ecstasy in Christian Perspective* = *In the House of the Lord: The Journey from Fear to Love* published 1986

1983-85, *Behold the Beauty of the Lord: Praying with Icons* published 1987

1983, January, becomes Professor of Divinity and Horace de Y. Lenz Lecturer at Harvard Divinity School

1983, May, stays in Mexico and Nicaragua

1983, August, visits Peru

1983, September-November, North American tour

1983, November-December, six week retreat at Trosly-Breuil, where he sees poster reproduction of Rembrandt's *Prodigal Son*

1984, Spring, lectures at Harvard Divinity School

1984, August-September, stays in Guatemala

1984, *Love in a Fearful Land: A Guatamalan Story* published 1985

1984, Christmas, thirty day retreat at Trosly-Breuil

1985, Spring, lectures at Harvard Divinity School

1985, March, visits Haiti

1985, 1 July, resigns from Harvard Divinity School

1985, Summer, teaches at Boston College

1985, August, to July, 1986, stays at Trosly-Breuil

1985-86, *The Road to Daybreak: A Spiritual Journey* published 1988

1985-86, *Heart Speaks to Heart: Three Gospel Meditations on Jesus* published 1989

1986, July, visits St Petersburg

1986, Early August, teaches at Boston College

1986, Late August to 1996, Pastor at L'Arche Daybreak, Richmond Hill, Ontario

1986, *Brieven aan Marc* published 1987

1987-88, *The Inner Voice of Love: The Journey through Anguish to Freedom* published 1996

1987-89, *In the Name of Jesus: Reflections on Christian Leadership* published 1989

1987-88, suffers breakdown at L'Arche Daybreak

1988, ET of *Brieven aan Marc* by Hubert Hoskins as *Letters to Marc about Jesus*

1988, *The Return of the Prodigal Son: A Story of Homecoming* published 1992

1988, *Jesus and Mary: Finding our Sacred Center* published 1993

1989, February, seriously hurt in road accident

1990, *Walk with Jesus*

1990, *Beyond the Mirror: Reflections on Death and Life*

1990, *Life of the Beloved: Spiritual Living in a Secular World*

1994, Autumn, teaches at Regis College, Toronto School of Theology

1994, *Our Greatest Gift: A Meditation on Dying and Caring*

1994, *Here and Now: Living in the Spirit*

1994, *With Burning Hearts: A Meditation on the Eucharistic Life*

1995, *Bread for the Journey: Reflections for Every Day of the Year* published 1996

1995, *Path Series: The Path of Freedom, The Path of Power, The Path of Peace*, and *The Path of Waiting* published posthumously as *Finding My Way Home* 2001

1995-96, *Can You Drink the Cup?* published 1996

1995-96, *Sabbatical Journey: The Diary of His Final Year* completed by Sue Mosteller and published 1998

1996, February, Adam Arnett dies

1996, *Adam: God's Beloved* completed by Sue Mosteller and published 1997

1996, Saturday, 21 September, dies, aged 64, after two heart attacks, in Hilversum

1996, 28 September, is buried in the Sacred Heart Cemetery, near Toronto

Short Titles

Books by and about Nouwen

(The short titles without surnames indicate books by Nouwen, whilst those with surnames preceding the short titles indicate books about Nouwen.)

Beauty Behold the Beauty of the Lord

Bengtson and Earnshaw, *Wheel* Turning the Wheel

Beumer, *Seeking* Henri Nouwen: A Restless Seeking for God

Bread Bread for the Journey

Burning With Burning Hearts

Clowning Clowning in Rome

Consolation A Letter of Consolation

Cry A Cry for Mercy

Cup Can You Drink the Cup?

Dear, *Peace* The Road to Peace

De Bono, *Exploration* An Exploration and Adaptation of Anton T. Boisen's Notion of the Psychiatric Chaplain in Responding to Current Issues in Clinical Chaplaincy

De Waal, *Seven* A Seven Day Journey with Thomas Merton

Durback, *Seeds* of Hope

Earnshaw, *Archives* The Henri J.M. Nouwen Archives and Research Collection

Encounters with Merton

Fearful Love in a Fearful Land

Ford, *Masters* Spiritual Masters for All Seasons

Ford, *Prophet* Wounded Prophet

Genesee The Genesee Diary

Gift Our Greatest Gift

Hands With Open Hands

Healer The Wounded Healer

Heart Speaks to Heart

Here and Now

Hernandez, *Integration* Henri Nouwen and Soul Care: A Ministry of Integration

Higgins, *Genius* Born of Anguish

History My History with God

House In the House of the Lord

Jesus and Mary

Jonas, *Beauty* of the Beloved

Journey Sabbatical Journey

LaNoue, *Legacy* The Spiritual Legacy of Henri Nouwen

Life of the Beloved

Lifesigns

Making All Things New

Marc Letters to Marc about Jesus

Memoriam In Memoriam

Merton Thomas Merton

Ministry Creative Ministry

Mirror Beyond the Mirror

Name In the Name of Jesus

O'Laughlin, *Beloved* God's Beloved

O'Laughlin, *Jesus*: A Gospel

O'Laughlin, *Vision* Henri Nouwen: His Life and Vision

Path Series: consists of *Freedom*, The Path of Freedom, *Peace* The Path of Peace, *Power* The Path of Power, and *Waiting* The Path of Waiting

Porter, *Befriending* Life

Pray to Live

Reaching Out

Reminder The Living Reminder

Return The Return of the Prodigal Son

Road The Road to Daybreak

Solitude Out of Solitude

Twomey and Pomerleau, *Remembering* Henri

Voice The Inner Voice of Love

Walk with Jesus

Way The Way of the Heart

Other Works

Edwards, *God* Van Gogh and God

Edwards, *Shoes* The Shoes of Van Gogh

Erickson, *Gate* At Eternity's Gate

Finley, *Palace* Merton's Palace of Nowhere

Harris, *Masterworks* The Masterworks of Van Gogh

Merkle, *Being Faithful* Being Faithful

Merton, *Conjectures* of a Guilty Bystander

Merton, *Mountain* The Seven Storey Mountain

Palmer, *Belly* In the Belly of a Paradox

Pramuk, *Sophia*

Schlabach, *Unlearning* Protestantism

Spink, *Universal* A Universal Heart

Van Gogh *Letters* The Letters of Vincent van Gogh

Vanier, *Together* Our Life Together

Bibliography

Primary Sources

Books

(A second date indicates the last revised edition published during Nouwen's lifetime.

Further dates indicate posthumous editions.)

Nouwen, Henri, J.M., *A Cry for Mercy: Prayers from the Genesee*, Garden City, NY: Doubleday, 1981, and Dublin: Gill and Macmillan, 1982, Maryknoll, NY: Orbis Books, 1994.

_____, *Adam: God's Beloved*, Completed by Sue Mosteller, Maryknoll, NY: Orbis, and London: Darton, Longman and Todd, 1997.

_____, *Aging: The Fulfillment of Life*, With Walter J. Gaffney, Garden City, NY: Doubleday, 1974, Garden City, NY: Doubleday, 1976, New York, NY: Doubleday, 1990.

_____, *A Letter of Consolation*, New York, NY: Harper and Row 1982, and Dublin: Gill and Macmillan, 1983, in *Making All Things New*, Grand Rapids, MI: Zondervan, 2000, and in *A Sorrow Shared*, Notre Dame, IN: Ave Maria Press, 2010.

_____, *Behold the Beauty of the Lord: Praying with Icons*, Notre Dame, IN: Ave Maria Press, 1987, 2007.

_____, *Beyond the Mirror: Reflections on Death and Life*, New York, NY: Crossroad, and London: Collins Fount, 1990, New York, NY: Crossroad, 2001.

_____, *Bread for the Journey: Reflections for Every Day of the Year*, London: Darton, Longman and Todd, 1996, and with the subtitle *A Daybook of Wisdom and Faith*, San Francisco, CA: HarperSanFrancisco, 1997.

_____, *Can You Drink the Cup?* Notre Dame, IN: Ave Maria Press, 1996.

_____, *Clowning in Rome: Reflections on Solitude, Celibacy, Prayer, and Contemplation*, Garden City, NY: Doubleday, 1979, Westminster, MD: Christian Classics, 1992. New York and Toronto: Doubleday, 2000, London: Darton, Longman and Todd, 2001.

_____, *Compassion: A Reflection on the Christian Life*, Co-authored with Donald P. McNeill and Douglas A. Morrison, London: Darton, Longman and Todd, and New York, NY: Doubleday, 1982, 2008.

_____, *Creative Ministry: Beyond Professionalism in Teaching, Preaching, Counselling, Organizing and Celebrating*, Garden City, NY: Doubleday, 1971, New York, NY: Doubleday, 1991.

_____, *Encounters with Merton*, New York, NY: Crossroad, 2004.

_____, *¡Gracias! A Latin American Journal*, San Francisco, CA: Harper & Row, 1983, Maryknoll, NY: Orbis, 1993.

_____, *Heart Speaks to Heart: Three Gospel Meditations on Jesus*, Notre Dame, IN: Ave Maria, 1989, 2007.

_____, *Here and Now: Living in the Spirit*, New York, NY: Crossroad, and London: Darton, Longman and Todd, 1994, 2003.

_____, *Home Tonight: Further Reflections on the Parable of the Prodigal Son*, New York, NY: Doubleday, and London: Darton, Longman and Todd, 2009.

_____, *In Memoriam*, Notre Dame, IN: Ave Maria Press, 1980, 2005.

_____, *In the Name of Jesus: Reflections on Christian Leadership*, New York, NY: Crossroad, and London: Darton, Longman and Todd, 1989.

_____, *Intimacy: Pastoral Psychological Essays*, Notre Dame, IN: Fides, 1969, with revised sub-title *Essays in Pastoral Psychology*, San Francisco, CA: Harper & Row, 1981, in *Making All Things New*, Grand Rapids, MI: Zondervan, 2000.

_____, *Jesus and Mary: Finding our Sacred Center*, Cincinnati, OH: St Anthony Messenger Press, 1993.

_____, English translation by Hubert Hoskins of *Brieven aan Marc*, Arnhem, Netherlands: Lannoo, 1988, as *Letters to Marc about Jesus*. San Francisco, CA: Harper & Row, and London: Darton, Longman and Todd, 1988, San Francisco, CA: Harper & Row, 1991.

_____, *Life of the Beloved: Spiritual Living in a Secular World*, New York, NY: Crossroad, 1992, London: Hodder & Stoughton, 1993.

_____, *Lifesigns: Intimacy, Fecundity, and Ecstasy in Christian Perspective = In the House of the Lord: The Journey from Fear to Love*, Garden City, NY: Doubleday, and London: Darton, Longman and Todd, 1986.

_____, *Love in a Fearful Land: A Guatamalan Story*, Notre Dame, IN: Ave Maria Press, 1985, Maryknoll, NY: Orbis, 2006.

_____, *Making All Things New: An Invitation to the Spiritual Life*, San Francisco, CA: HarperSanFrancisco, and Dublin: Gill and Macmillan, 1981, in *Making All Things New*, Grand Rapids, MI: Zondervan, 2000.

_____, *Our Greatest Gift: A Meditation on Dying and Caring*, San Francisco, CA: HarperSanFrancisco, and London: Hodder and Stoughton, 1994.

_____, *Out of Solitude: Three Meditations on the Christian Life*, Notre Dame, IN: Ave Maria, 1974, 2004.

_____, *Path Series: The Path of Freedom, The Path of Power, The Path of Peace, and The Path of Waiting*, New York: Crossroad, and London: Darton, Longman and Todd, 1995.

_____, *Peacework: Prayer, Resistance, Community*, Maryknoll, NY: Orbis Books, 2005.

_____, English translation by David Schlaver of *Bidden om het Leven* Bilthoven: Amboboeken, 1970, with assistance by Henri Nouwen as *Pray to Live*, Notre Dame, IN: Fides, 1972. Second edition *Thomas Merton: Contemplative Critic*, San Francisco, CA: HarperSanFrancisco, 1981.

Third edition *Thomas Merton: Contemplative Critic*, Liguori, MO.: Triumph Books, 1991. Fourth edition *Encounters with Merton*, New York: Crossroad, 2004.

_____, *Reaching Out: The Three Movements of the Spiritual Life*, New York: Doubleday, 1975, London: Collins, 1976, Garden City, NY: Image Books, 1986, London: Font, 1998.

_____, *Sabbatical Journey: The Diary of His Final Year*, Completed by Sue Mosteller, New York: Crossroad, and London: Darton, Longman and Todd, 1998.

_____, *The Genesee Diary: Report from a Trappist Monastery*, Garden City, NY: Doubleday, 1976, London: Darton, Longman and Todd, 1995, 2008.

_____, *The Inner Voice of Love: The Journey through Anguish to Freedom*, New York: Doubleday, 1996, and London: Darton, Longman and Todd, 1997.

_____, *The Living Reminder: Service and Prayer in Memory of Jesus Christ*, San Francisco, CA: HarperSanFrancisco, 1977, Dublin: Gill and Macmillan, 1982.

_____, *The Return of the Prodigal Son: A Meditation on Fathers, Brothers and Sons*, New York, NY: Doubleday, and with new subtitle *A Story of Homecoming*, London: Darton, Longman and Todd, 1992, New York, NY: Continuum, 1995.

_____, *The Road to Daybreak: A Spiritual Journey*, New York: Doubleday, 1988, London: Darton, Longman and Todd, 1989.

_____, *The Selfless Way of Christ: Downward Mobility and the Spiritual Life*, Maryknoll, NY: Orbis Books, 2007.

_____, *The Way of the Heart: Desert Spirituality and Contemporary Ministry*, New York, NY: Seabury Press, and London: Darton, Longman and Todd, 1981.

_____, *The Wounded Healer: Ministry in Contemporary Society*, Garden City, NY: Doubleday, 1972, London: Darton, Longman and Todd, 1994.

_____, *Walk with Jesus: Stations of the Cross*, Maryknoll, NY: Orbis, 1990.

_____, *With Burning Hearts: A Meditation on the Eucharistic Life*, Maryknoll, NY: Orbis, and London: Geoffrey Chapman, 1994, Maryknoll, NY: Orbis 2003.

_____, English translation by Patrick Gaffney of *Met Open Handen*, Bilthoven: Amboboeken, 1971, as *With Open Hands*, Notre Dame, IN: Ave Maria, 1972, Notre Dame, IN: Ave Maria, 1995, 2005.

Compilations

Dear, John, ed., *The Road to Peace*, Maryknoll, NY: Orbis Books, 1998.

Durback, Robert, ed., *A Retreat with Henri Nouwen: Reclaiming our Humanity*, London: Darton, Longman and Todd, 2003.

_____, *Henri Nouwen: In My Own Words*, Liguori, MO: Liguori, 2001, London: Darton, Longman and Todd, 2002.

_____, *Seeds of Hope*, New York: Bantam, 1989 and London: Darton, Longman and Todd, revised edition, 1998.

Ford, Michael, ed., *Arrivals and Departures: The Restless World of Henri J.M. Nouwen*, London: Darton, Longman and Todd, 2007, published in the USA as *A Restless Soul: Meditations from the Road*, Notre Dame, IN: Ave Maria Press, 2008.

_____, *The Dance of Life: Weaving Sorrows and Blessings into One Joyful Step*, Published in the U.K. as *Spiritual Direction with Henri Nouwen*, Notre Dame, IN: Ave Maria Press and London: Darton, Longman and Todd, 2005.

_____, *Eternal Seasons: A Liturgical Journey with Henri Nouwen*, Notre Dame, IN: Sorin Books and London: Darton, Longman and Todd, 2003.

Garvey, John, ed., *Circles of Love: Daily Readings with Henri Nouwen*, Springfield, IL.: Templegate and London: Darton, Longman and Todd, 1988.

Johna, Franz with Henri Nouwen, eds., *Zeige mir den Weg: Text für alle Tage von Aschermittwoch bis Ostern*, Freiburg: Herder, 1990, English translation *Show Me the Way: Readings for Each Day of Lent*, New York, NY: Crossroad, 1992, and London: Darton, Longman and Todd, 1993.

Jonas, Robert A., ed., *Henri Nouwen: Writings selected with an Introduction by Robert A. Jonas*, Published in the U.K. as *Beauty of the Beloved: A Henri J.M. Nouwen Anthology*, Maryknoll, NY: Orbis, 1998, London: Darton, Longman and Todd, 1999.

Mosteller, Sue, ed., *Finding My Way Home: Pathways to Life and the Spirit: The Path of Power, The Path of Peace, The Path of Waiting, The Path of Living and Dying*, Foreword by Wendy Wilson Greer, with Preface by Sue Mosteller, New York, NY: Crossroad, 2001.

Articles

Nouwen, Henri. J.M., 'Adam's Peace,' *World Vision*, August-September, 1988, 4-7.

_____, 'Celibacy,' *Pastoral Psychology* 27/2, Winter, 1978, 79-90.

_____, 'Compassion: Solidarity, Consolation, and Comfort,' *America*, 13 March, 1976, 195-200.

_____, 'Contemplation and Ministry,' *Sojourners* 7, June, 1978, 9-12.

_____, *Hospitality*, Pine City, NY: *Monastic Studies* #10, Easter, 1974, 1-28.

_____, 'The Trusting Heart & The Primacy of the Mystical Life', *New Oxford Review*, October, 1986

_____, 'Unceasing Prayer,' *America* July 29-August 5, 1978, 46-51.

Forewords, Introductions, Prefaces, and Afterwords to Books

De Waal, Esther, *A Seven Day Journey with Thomas Merton*, Foreword by Henri Nouwen, Guildford: Eagle, 1992.

Dufresne, Edward R., *Partnership: Marriage and the Committed Life*, Foreword by Henri Nouwen, New York and Toronto: Paulist, 1975.

Edwards, Cliff, *Van Gogh and God: A Creative Spiritual Quest*, Foreword by Henri Nouwen, Chicago, IL: Loyola University Press, 1989.

Finley, James, *Merton's Palace of Nowhere: A Search for God through Awareness of the True Self*, Foreword by Henri Nouwen, Notre Dame, IN: Ave Maria Press, 1978.

Francis de Sales and Jane de Chantal, *Letters of Spiritual Direction*, ET Peronne Marie Thibert, selected and ed., Wendy M. Wright and Joseph F. Power, Preface by Henri Nouwen, New York, NY: Paulist (Classics of Western Spirituality Series), 1988.

Br Lawrence, *Practice of the Presence of God*, English translation John J. Delaney, Foreword by Henri Nouwen, New York and Toronto: Image Books, 1977.

Merton, Thomas, *Life and Holiness*, Introduction by Henri Nouwen, Gethsemani, KY: The Abbey of Gethsemani, 1963, 1996 edition.

Okhuijsen, Gijs, *In Heaven there are no Thunderstorms: Celebrating the Liturgy with Developmentally Disabled People*, Foreword by Henri Nouwen, Collegeville, MN: Liturgical Press, 1992.

Palmer, Parker J., *In the Belly of a Paradox: A Celebration of Contradictions in the Thought of Thomas Merton*, Foreword by Henri Nouwen, Wallingford, PA: Pendle Hill Publications, 1979.

_____, *The Promise of Paradox: A Celebration of Contradictions in the Christian Life*, Introduction by Henri Nouwen, Notre Dame, IN: Ave Maria Press, 1981.

Philippe, Thomas, *The Contemplative Life*, ET Carmine Buonaiuto, ed. Edward D. O'Connor, Forewords by Henri Nouwen and Jean Vanier, New York, NY: Crossroad, 1990.

Romero, Oscar A., *The Violence of Love*, Compiled and ET James R.Brockman, Foreword by Henri Nouwen, Farmington, PA: Plough House, orig. ed. San Francisco, CA: HarperSanFrancisco, 1998.

Vanier, Jean, *From Brokenness to Community*, Foreword by Henri Nouwen, Mahwah, NJ: Paulist Press, 1992.

_____, *Man and Woman He Made Them*, Foreword by Henri Nouwen, Toronto: Anglican Book Centre, and London: Darton, Longman and Todd, 1985.

Chapters in Books

Oberholtzer, W. Dwight, ed., *Is Gay Good? Ethics, Theology and Homosexuality*, Philadelphia: Westminster Press, 1971, chapter 10, pp. 204-12.

Manuscripts

Nouwen, Henri J.M., *Introduction to the Spiritual Life*, Harvard University, 1983, Handout 14.

_____, *My History with God* Regis College, the Jesuit Graduate Faculty of Theology, a member institution of the Toronto School of Theology, within the University of Toronto, Autumn, 1994.

(The Henri J.M. Nouwen Archives and Research Collection at the John M. Kelly Library, University of St Michael's College in the University of Toronto, publishes a Finding Guide to the material in the Archives and Collection, which may be accessed online at stmikes.utoronto. ca/kelly/nouwen/finding-guide.asp)

Secondary Sources

Books

Barth, Karl, *Church Dogmatics*, Edinburgh: T. and T. Clark, 1956.

Bengtson, Jonathan and Gabrielle Earnshaw, eds., *Turning the Wheel: Henri Nouwen and Our Search for God*, Maryknoll, NY: Orbis Books, 2007.

Beumer, Jurjen, *Onrustig zoeken naar God. De spiritualiteit van Henri Nouwen*, Tielt: Lannoo, 1996, ET by David E. Schlaver and Nancy Forest-Flier as *Henri Nouwen: A Restless Seeking for God*, New York, NY: Crossroad, 1997.

Billy, Dennis, *Under the Starry Night*, Notre Dame, IN: Ave Maria Press, 1997.

Bonhoeffer, Dietrich, *Life Together*, New York, NY: Harpers, 1954.

Earnshaw, Gabrielle, *The Henri J. M. Nouwen Archives and Research Collection*, Toronto: John M. Kelly Library, University of St Michael's College, 2011.

Edwards, Cliff, *The Shoes of Van Gogh: A Spiritual and Artistic Journey to the Ordinary*, New York, NY: Crossroad, 2004.

Erickson, Kathleen Powers, *At Eternity's Gate: The Spiritual Vision of Vincent van Gogh*, Grand Rapids, MI, and Cambridge: William B. Eerdmans, 1998.

Ford, Michael, *Wounded Prophet: A Portrait of Henri J.M. Nouwen*, London: Darton, Longman and Todd, 1999. Revised edition 2006.

_____, *Spiritual Masters For All Seasons*, New York, NY, and Mahwah, NJ: Paulist Press, 2009.

Harris, Nathaniel, *The Masterworks of Van Gogh*, Bristol: Parragon, 1997, r1998.

Hernandez, Wil, *Henri Nouwen: A Spirituality of Imperfection*, Mahwah, NJ: Paulist Press, 2006.

_____, *Henri Nouwen and Soul Care: A Ministry of Integration*, Mahwah, NJ: Paulist Press, 2008.

_____, *Henri Nouwen and Spiritual Polarities*, Mahwah, NJ: Paulist Press, 2012.

Higgins, Michael W., *Genius Born of Anguish: The Life and Legacy of Henri Nouwen*, Mahwah, NJ: Paulist Press, 2012.

Jung, Carl, *Memories, Dreams, Reflections*, London: Fontana, 1995.

LaNoue, Deirdre, *The Spiritual Legacy of Henri Nouwen*, New York, NY: Continuum, 2001.

Marcus, Paul, *In Search of the Spiritual: Gabriel Marcel, Psychoanalysis, and the Sacred*, London, Karnak Books, 2013.

Merkle, Judith A., *Being Faithful: Christian Commitment in Modern Society*, London and New York, NY: Continuum, 2010.

Merton, Thomas, *An Introduction to Christian Mysticism: Initiation into the Monastic Tradition 3*, ed. Patrick O'Connell, Kalamazoo, , Garden City, NY: Doubleday, 1966.

_____, *Conjectures of a Guilty Bystander*, Garden City, NY: Doubleday, 1966.

_____, *Learning to Love: The Journals of Thomas Merton*, vol. 6, 1966-1967, ed. Christine M. Bochen, San Francisco, CA: HarperSanFrancisco, 1998.

_____, *Love and Living*, ed. Naomi Burton Stone and Patrick Hart, New York, NY: Farrar, Straus and Giroux, 1979, New York: Harcourt Brace Jovanovich, 1985.

_____, *Nanae No Yama*, Tokyo: Tokyo Publishing Company, 1965.

_____, *New Seeds of Contemplation*, Norfolk, CT: New Directions, 1961.

_____, *Raids on the Unspeakable*, New York, NY: New Directions, 1966.

_____, *The Behavior of Titans*, New York, NY: New Directions, 1961.

_____, *The Hidden Ground of Love: The Letters of Thomas Merton on Religious Experience and Social Concerns*, ed. William H. Shannon, New York, NY: Farrar, Straus and Giroux, 1985.

_____, *The Literary Essays of Thomas Merton*, ed. Patrick Hart, New York, NY: New Directions, 1981.

_____, *The New Man*, New York, NY: Farrar, Straus and Cudahy, 1961, New York, NY: Farrar, Straus and Giroux, 1999.

_____, *The Seven Storey Mountain*, New York, NY: Harcourt Brace, 1948, New York: Harcourt Brace Jovanovich, 1999.

Miller, J. Michael CSB, ed. *The Encyclicals of John Paul II*, Huntington, IN: Our Sunday Visitor, 1996.

Nouwen, Laurent J.M., *Henri's vader vertelt: Zo maar een verhaal over een doorsnee-katholiek gezin uit de eerste helft van deze eeuw waarvan de eerstgeboren zoon bereids in zijn prille jeugd blijk gaf van zijn passie voor het priesterschap* (Henri's father speaks: just the story of an average Catholic family from the first half of this century whose first-born son showed signs of a passion for the priesthood, even in his tenderest years), privately printed and distributed within a small circle.

O'Laughlin, Michael, *God's Beloved: A Spiritual Biography of Henri Nouwen*, Maryknoll, NY: Orbis, 2004.

_____, *Henri Nouwen: His Life and Vision*, Maryknoll, NY: Orbis Books, Toronto: Novalis and London: Darton, Longman and Todd, 2005.

Phillips, Vera and Edwin Robinson, *JB Phillips: Wounded Healer*, Grand Rapids, MI: Eerdmans, 1985.

Porter, Beth, ed. with Susan M.S. Brown and Philip Coulter, *Befriending Life: Encounters with Henri Nouwen*, New York, NY: Doubleday and London: Darton, Longman and Todd, 2001.

Pramuk, Christopher, *Sophia: The Hidden Christ of Thomas Merton*, Collegeville, PA: Liturgical Press, 2009.

Ringma, Charles R., *The Seeking Heart: A Journey with Henri Nouwen*, Brewster, MA: Paraclete Press, 2006.

Schlabach, Gerald, *Unlearning Protestantism: Sustaining Christian Community in an Unstable Age*, Grand Rapids, MI: Brazos Press, 2010.

Spink, Kathryn, *A Universal Heart: The Life and Vision of Brother Roger of Taizé*, London: SPCK, 1986, 2nd edition, 2005.

Sund, Judy, *True to Temperament: Van Gogh and French Naturalist Literature*, New York, NY: Cambridge University Press, 1992.

Twomey, Gerald S. and Claude Pomerleau, eds., *Remembering Henri: The Life and Legacy of Henri Nouwen*, Maryknoll, NY: Orbis Books and Toronto: Novalis, 2006.

Van Gogh, Vincent, *The Letters of Vincent van Gogh*, ed. Pomerans, Arnold and Ronald de Leeuw, London: Penguin Classics, 1997.

Vanier, Jean, *A Wound Deep in Man's Heart*, Toronto: Daybreak Publications, 1981.

_____, *Our Life Together: A Memoir in Letters*, London: Darton, Longman and Todd, 2008.

Vanier, Thérèse, *One Bread, One Body: The Ecumenical Experience of L'Arche*, Leominster: Gracewing and Ottawa: Novalis, 1997.

Young, Frances M., *God's Presence: A Contemporary Recapitulation of Early Christianity* (*Current Issues in Theology*), Cambridge: Cambridge University Press, 2013.

Articles

Argan, Glen, 'Nouwen finds a home,' *Western Catholic Reporter*, 21 March, 1994, 6.

Boers, Arthur, 'Faces of Faith: Henri Nouwen,' *The Other Side*, September/October, 1989, 14-19.

Coady, Mary Frances, 'Nouwen Finds Rest at Daybreak,' *Catholic New Times*, 23 November, 1986, 3.

Gardner, Fiona, *The Only Mind Worth Having: Thomas Merton and the Child Mind*, Cambridge: Lutterworth Press, 2016.

Goulet, Yvonne, 'Father Nouwen on Nicaragua,' *The Church World*, 29 September, 1983, 3, 12-13.

Grainger, Brett, 'Henri: A Heart's Desire,' *Sojourners* 25, November-December, 1966, 26-30.

Greene, Amy, 'An Interview with Catholic Priest Writer Henri Nouwen,' *SBC Today*, September, 1990, 10-11.

Hiltner, Seward, 'Henri J.M. Nouwen: Pastoral Theologian of the Year,' *Pastoral Psychology* 27:1, Fall, 1978, 4-7.

Kravalis, Gunar, 'At Home with Henri Nouwen – A Visit to Daybreak,' *The Presbyterian Record*, April, 1989, 23-25.

McFarland, John, 'The Minister as Narrator,' *The Christian Ministry*, 18:1, January, 1987, 20.

Meehan, Francis X., 'He Pleads, Knowing the Charge to Come,' *The Philadelphia Inquirer*, 13 August, 1983, A9.

Odell, Catherine, 'Father Nouwen Sees the Light at Daybreak,' *Our Sunday Visitor*, 12 July, 1992, 5

O'Laughlin, Michael, 'Henri Nouwen in Life and Death,' *America* 163, 10 May, 1997, 18-20.

Penkett, Luke, 'Arrivals and Departures: The Restless World of Henri Nouwen' (Book Review), *Ministry Today*, 42, March, 2008.

_____, 'Thomas Merton: Master of Attention' (Book Review), *Ministry Today*, 42, March, 2008.

_____, 'Behold the Beauty of the Lord: Praying with Icons' (Book Review), *Ministry Today*, 44, September, 2008.

_____, 'Home Tonight: Further Reflections on the Parable of the Prodigal Son' (Book Review), *Ministry Today*, 48, March, 2010.

_____, 'The Genesee Diary' and 'Peacework' (Book Reviews), *The Heythrop Journal*, 51:3, May, 2010, 536-38.

_____, 'Unlearning Protestantism' (Book Review), *Ministry Today*, 55, July, 2012.

_____, 'Reshaping Ecumenical Theology: The Church Made Whole? Paul Avis' (Book Review) *The Heythrop Journal*, 53:6, November, 2012, 1061-62.

_____, 'Our Life Together: A Memoir in Letters' and 'Essential Writings: Jean Vanier' (Book Reviews), *The Heythrop Journal*, 54:3, May, 2013, 530-31.

_____, 'A Nouwen Trilogy' (Book Review), *Ministry Today*, 58, August, 2013.

_____, 'In Search of the Spiritual' (Book Review), *The Heythrop Journal*, 55:2, May, 2014, 323.

_____, 'Genius Born of Anguish' (Book Review), *The Heythrop Journal*, 55:2, May, 2014, 340-41.

Renner, Gerald, 'Modern-day "Saint" Reflects on Works, Life,' *The Hartford Courant*, 14 October, 1993, Connecticut page, Section B.

Todd, Douglas, 'In Weakness There is Strength,' *The Weekend Sun*, 16 April, 1994, D15.

Uhler, Mary C., 'From Harvard to l'Arche: Henri Nouwen Shares His Journey,' *Catholic Herald*, 23 July, 1987, 1, 3.

Vesey, John E., 'Nouwen's Difficult Journey,' *The Tablet*, 19 May, 1983, 3.

Wakefield, Dan, 'Spiritual Impact: Encounters with Henri Nouwen,' *Christian Century* 114, 19-26 March, 1997, 301-3.

Witvoet, Bert, 'Profile,' *Calvinist Contact*, 23 October, 1987, 10-11.

Unpublished Writings

Boers, 'From the House of Fear to the House of Love: An Encounter with Henri Nouwen,' unpublished, n.d. Henri Nouwen Archives, Yale Divinity School Library, now in The Henri J. M. Nouwen Archives and Research Collection, John M. Kelly Library, University of St Michael's College, University of Toronto.

Theses

De Bono, Christopher E., 'An Exploration and Adaptation of Anton T. Boisen's Notion of the Psychiatric Chaplain in Responding to Current Issues in Clinical Chaplaincy,' PhD thesis, Faculty of Theology of the University of St Michael's College and the Pastoral Department of the Toronto School of Theology, September, 2012.

Henderson, Kyle L., 'The Reformation of Pastoral Theology in the Life of Henri J.M. Nouwen,' PhD thesis, Southwestern Baptist Theological Seminary, 1994.

Kisner, Jeffrey Allan, 'Self-Disclosing Stories in Sermons: A Multidisciplinary Rationale,' PhD thesis, The Southern Baptist Theological Seminary, 1989.

Penkett, Luke, 'Finding One Another in Christ: Ecumenism in the Life and Writing of Henri J. M. Nouwen', PhD thesis, Lambeth Palace, London, 2013.

DVDs

Angels over the Net, Producer: Isabelle Steyart, and Director: Bart Gavigan, 30 minutes, Toronto, Ontario: Spark Productions, 1995.

Journey of the Heart: The Life of Henri Nouwen. Producer and Director: Karen Pascal, 60 minutes, Markham, Ontario: Windbourne Productions, 2006.

Endnotes

Introduction

1   Although Anton Boisen's influence on Nouwen is indisputable, for instance, he is not included for discussion here as a mentor because, unlike Merton, Van Gogh, Vanier and Rembrandt, Nouwen, having completed his studies on Boisen, does not return to reflect specifically on him later in his ministry or writing.

2   There are brief but, at times, penetrating passages on Merton in: Bengtson and Earnshaw, *Wheel*, 57-67; Ford, *Prophet*, 130-32; Higgins, *Genius*, 41-44; O'Laughlin, *Beloved*, 105-9; and O'Laughlin, *Vision*, 67-69; on Van Gogh in Bengtson and Earnshaw, *Wheel*, 111-21; O'Laughlin, *Beloved*, 97-105; O'Laughlin, *Vision*, 81-83; and Twomey and Pomerleau, *Remembering*, 105-18; on Vanier in Ford, *Prophet*, 160-64 and 167-68; and O'Laughlin, *Vision*, 105-09; and on Rembrandt in Ford, *Prophet*, 184-86; O'Laughlin, *Vision*, 140-42; and Twomey and Pomerleau, *Remembering*, 105-18.

3   By 'primary writing' I mean the thirty-nine books, known as the Henri Nouwen corpus, that Nouwen had written and intended to be published in book form in English during his lifetime, including those he was working on in 1996 that were incomplete and published in book form posthumously. Details of articles, chapters, forewords, introductions, and prefaces written by Nouwen that are incorporated into other writers' books, and published compilations of Nouwen's writing, papers presented at professional meetings, addresses, homilies, and speeches, and manu-/typescripts, where they were used in the preparation of the thesis, are included in its bibliography and need not be repeated here.

4   During his life time, Nouwen did not officially authorise any biographies nor, with the exception of a short unpublished synopsis of his life entitled 'My History with God' written in 1994 for a class he was teaching in Toronto, did he undertake to write his own autobiography. The five standard biographies, in order of publication, are: Beumer, *Onrustig zoeken naar God. De spiritualiteit van Henri Nouwen*, ET by Schlaver and Forest-Flier as *Henri Nouwen: A Restless Seeking for God* (note that this first biography of Nouwen was written by a Dutch Protestant); Ford, *Wounded Prophet: A Portrait of Henri J.M. Nouwen* (note that Ford, also, is an Anglican); LaNoue, *The Spiritual Legacy of Henri Nouwen* (note that LaNoue, too, is a Baptist); O'Laughlin, *God's Beloved: A Spiritual Biography of Henri Nouwen* (the first biography of Nouwen to be written by a Roman Catholic); and O'Laughlin, *Henri Nouwen: His Life and Vision*. In 2009, the Henri Nouwen Legacy Trust contracted Roman Catholic scholar Michael W. Higgins to write an authorised biography, at which he is currently working. A prolegomenon of this, *Genius Born of Anguish: The Life and Legacy of Henri Nouwen*, was published by the Paulist Press in 2012.

5   Beumer, *Seeking*, 132.

6   *Compassion*, 4.

7   Ibid., xi.

8   Idem.

9   Idem.

10   *Compassion*, 7.

11   Ibid., 8.

12   It is remarkable that the three Roman Catholic writers should choose the words of a major Protestant theologian for such a key description in their book *Compassion* rather than those of a Roman Catholic one.

13   Barth, *Church Dogmatics*, IV/1, 190, quoted in *Compassion*, 25.

14   *Compassion*, 28.
15   Ibid., 29.

Chapter 1: Thomas Merton, monk, contemplative, poet

1   O'Laughlin, *Beloved*, 105.
2   In 1966 Dr John Dos Santos (a colleague with whom Henri Nouwen had worked in the field of religion and psychiatry at the Menninger Clinic, Topeka, Kansas from 1964 to 1966) was invited to set up a psychology department at the University of Notre Dame, Indiana. Nouwen agreed to teach there for two semesters. In fact, Fr Theodore Hesburgh, Notre Dame's president, insisted that Nouwen remain and he stayed for two years, until 1968.
3   Nouwen began lecturing on themes of confusion, depression, intimacy and love, and his audiences soon asked for copies of his lectures. In one of his audiences was a journalist from the *National Catholic Reporter* who sought permission to put one of these lectures into print. The interest in the article was so great that Nouwen was invited to submit more articles from his lectures. Out of this collection came his first book, *Intimacy: Essays in Pastoral Psychology*.
      In his Acknowledgements, Nouwen writes, '[*Intimacy*] is born out of a two-year "visit" to the University of Notre Dame.' Published in 1969, it was reprinted in 1981 with the revised sub-title *Essays in Pastoral Psychology*. In the first run of *Intimacy* Nouwen included a passage on homosexual love. He removed this from the first re-print later in 1969 and from all subsequent reprints and editions because, as he confesses in Oberholtzer's *Is Gay Good?*, 'many homosexuals [told me] that I was wrong or at least one-sided, since most of my impressions came from my practice as a psychologist', 204.
4   *Creative Ministry: Beyond Professionalism in Teaching, Preaching, Counselling, Organizing and Celebrating*, was published in 1971, and reprinted in 1978 and again in 1991. It was re-issued with a revised text in 2003. The theme of this second book is 'the relationship between professionalism and spirituality in the ministry' and is a book whose teaching is still pertinent today. It was a much-needed contribution to the field of pastoral care, integrating psychology and pastoral.' Such an approach (applying psychology to pastoral care) was ahead of its time.
5   There is a comparative dearth of information on Nouwen during the years 1968-70. The Henri Nouwen Archives intend to fill this lacuna in the coming years, and plans include collecting copies of documents from Dutch institutions that Nouwen attended or worked for at this time.
6   *Bidden om het Leven, Het Contemplatief engagement van Thomas Merton*, Bilthoven: Amboboeken, 1970; *Pray to Live*, Notre Dame, IN: Fides, 1972; 2nd ed. *Thomas Merton: Contemplative Critic*, San Francisco, CA: HarperSanFrancisco, 1981; 3rd ed. *Thomas Merton: Contemplative Critic*, Liguori, MO: Triumph Books, 1991; 4th ed. *Encounters with Merton: Spiritual Reflections*, New York: Crossroad, 2004. Nouwen was to return to the subject of Thomas Merton in writing his Foreword to Palmer, *Belly*.
7   *Mit Open Handen* was published in 1971. Two years later the English version was published as *With Open Hands*, translated by Patrick Gaffney, and was reprinted in 1985. A revised edition appeared in 1994, and a second revised edition in 2006.
8   *Pray*, 3.
9   Idem.
10   From Bamberger's Preface to *Pray*, viii.
11   For an early 'psychologically penetrative bit of analysis found in a correspondence of November 28, 1965, at which time Bamberger was a monk of the Abbey of Gethsemani, Kentucky, and Nouwen was still at the Menninger Clinic in Kansas, Father John Eudes reveals Nouwen to himself, identifies the dangerous dynamic that governs Nouwen's life, cautions the young Dutch priest to address the tensions that threaten to sunder him spiritually and emotionally, and provides ample evidence that his counsel will be determinate for some time to come,' see Higgins, *Genius*, 40-41. Higgins himself comments that this is 'an extraordinarily accurate assessment of Nouwen's inner struggles,' 41.
12   Bamberger's Preface to *Pray*, ix.
13   Higgins, *Genius*, 42.
14   *Encounters*, 75.
15   Letter from Nouwen to Annet van Lindenberg, quoted in Beumer, *Seeking*, 179 n. 13. van Lindenberg is the writer of a master's thesis titled 'Weest stil, enweet ..., De betekenis van het werk van Henri J.M. Nouwen voor de praktijk van het protestantse pastoraat'(Be Still and Know ..., The meaning of the work of Henri J. M. Nouwen for the practice of Protestant ministry), Theologische Universiteit, Kampen, 1988, unpublished.
16   Ford, *Masters*, 91. However, in the same letter from Nouwen to van Lindenberg, he writes that, although Merton had a great influence on him, it was 'probably more through his personality than through what he wrote.'

17   Christine M. Bochen ed., *Learning to Love*, vol. 6, 232.
18   Gabrielle Earnshaw in a private communication alerts me to the discrepancy between the names of those who met with Merton and Nouwen. Whilst Merton mentions Raymond and Alexis, Nouwen refers, in his Foreword to De Waal's *Seven*, to Joe Ahearn, 9.
19   Ford, *Masters*, 91. Nouwen was later to describe the encounter as 'unspectacular' in his Foreword to Finley, *Palace*. 7.
20   *Pray*, 3.
21   Finley, *Palace*, 7.
22   Nouwen's Foreword to De Waal, *Seven*, 9-10.
23   Merton, *Life and Holiness*, 1996 edition, 3.
24   Colin Wilbur Williams, a Methodist Church Minister, served as Dean of Yale Divinity School from 1969 to 1979. One of his first aims at Yale was to secure Nouwen as a member of faculty.
25   On Nouwen at Yale, see Beumer, *Seeking*, 32-35; O'Laughlin, *Vision*, 63-66; and Ford, *Prophet*, 115-26.
26   On Nouwen's loyalty to the Roman Catholic Church in the Netherlands, see O'Laughlin, *Vision*, 63; and Ford, *Prophet*, 114.
27   Quoted in Ford, *Prophet*, 116-17.
28   Merton, *Conjectures*, 21. Merton's entry in his diary for March 19, 1958, Feast of St Joseph, has a number of significant differences of detail.
29   *Pray*, x.
30   Merton was to live for a further three years, dying on 10 December, 1968, years that were spent as a solitary in a hermitage at Gethsemani. *Pray*, 39.
31   *Pray*, 46-47.
32   Palmer, *Belly*, 3, 4.
33   Higgins, *Genius*, 45.
34   O'Laughlin, *Beloved*, 105.
35   Higgins, *Genius*, 45.
36   Among Nouwen's biographers, only Jurjen Beumer, Deidre LaNoue, and Michael A. Ford discuss compassion in the context of Nouwen's life and writing. Of these, Beumer and Ford concentrate on *Compassion* the book, whilst LaNoue is wider ranging.
37   McNeill and Morrison undertook a limited revision of *Compassion* in the first decade of the present century, making the book more gender-sensitive in the way it speaks of God '[in] the spirit of Henri Nouwen and by many readers who expressed their appreciation for this kind of sensitivity, and this revised edition was published in 2008, that is, twelve years after Nouwen's death. In their Preface to this edition they write, 'Although the world has changed immensely from 1982 to the present, *Compassion* has continued to speak to a new audience in each of these twenty-two intervening years. This is a great tribute to Henri Nouwen who, although he predeceased the other authors, lives on in *Compassion* as he does in his many books' (xiii).
38   The publication of *The Seven Storey Mountain* was a catalyst to a vast variety of people's correspondence with Merton. In the 1940s the monks at Gethsemani were allowed to correspond on only four occasions in the whole year. By the 1960s this had changed.
39   Merton, *Mountain*, 11.
40   *Pray*, 67.
41   O'Laughlin, *Vision*, 69.
42   Finley, *Palace*, 8.
43   *Pray*, 9.
44   Genesee Abbey was founded in 1951.
45   O'Laughlin, *Vision*, 72.
46   Ibid., 74. Italics added. On Nouwen and monastic spirituality, see Ford, *Masters*, 94-95.
47   Ford, *Masters*, 98.
48   Ibid., 124-25.
49   The 'Fourth and Walnut' experience took place when Merton was in Louisville for a doctor's appointment in 1958. He saw a great mix of people and was overwhelmed by his feelings of oneness with them. Fourth Street, named '4th Street' in Merton's time, is a busy street. Its intersection with Walnut, more recently named Muhammad Ali Street, is a busy one. The area has been re-named Thomas Merton Square. Near the Roman Catholic Cathedral of Louisville, it is a focus of nightclubs and restaurants.
50   Merton recorded the first account in his diary journal written the next day. The second, in his *Conjectueres*, has some significant alterations.
51   Merton, *Conjectures*, 140-41.
52   Idem.

53 O'Laughlin, *Vision*, 70.
54 Merton, *Conjectures*, 140. Nouwen repeats Merton's description in the entry for 11 August, 1974, *Genesee*, 87. Nouwen had also written on the subject in *Reaching*, 41-44, also completed at the Genesee.
55 Merton, *Conjectures*, 141.
56 Idem.
57 Merton, *New Seeds of Contemplation*, 123-24, quoted in *Reaching*, 116.
58 *Reminder*, 51.
59 Ibid., 15. Second edition has 'God's commitment to live in solidarity with us.'
60 Idem.
61 *Compassion*, 15. Second edition has 'Jesus was the concrete embodiment ... Jesus' divine compassion.'
62 Ibid., 16.
63 Idem.
64 *Compassion*, 18.
65 *House*, 41.
66 Ibid., 16.
67 Ibid. Second edition has 'where his most intimate and intense emotions are located.'
68 The verb is related to *rachamim*, the Hebrew word for compassion, which is used when referring to the womb of God.
69 Beumer, *Seeking*, 133.
70 *Compassion*, 3.
71 Idem.
72 *Compassion*, 4.
73 Idem.
74 Beumer, *Seeking*, 133.
75 Idem.
76 *House*, 21.
77 Idem.
78 On 'voluntary displacement' see Nouwen, 'Contemplation and Action,' sermon preached at St Paul's Church, Columbia University 10 December, 1978, on the tenth anniversary of Thomas Merton's death, published in Dear, *Peace*, 195-200.
79 Finley, *Palace*, 8.
80 *Way*, 39.
81 Ibid., 40.
82 *Compassion*, 65.
83 Nouwen, *Introduction to the Spiritual Life*, Harvard University, 1983, Handout 14.
84 *Nanae No Yama*, quoted in *Pray*, 68.
85 *Compassion*, 8.
86 *Reaching Out*, 20 (1998 edition).
87 Nouwen, 'Thomas Merton's Call to Contemplation and Action,' in Dear, *Peace*, 195-200.
88 *Compassion*, 116-17.
89 Ibid, 117-18.
90 *Compassion*, 79.
91 Ibid., 81.
92 Dear, *Peace*, 196-97.
93 Ibid., 82. The second edition has 'the compassionate Christ is made manifest and a healing presence is given to all.'
94 O'Laughlin, *Beloved*, 107-8.
95 *The Sign of Jonas* 325-26 quoted in *Reaching*, 58.
96 *Pray*, 47. Italics added.
97 *Pray*, 48.
98 Ibid., 47.
99 *Reaching*, 58.
100 Finley, *Palace*, 9. Finley's book, *Palace*, is, similarly, not primarily about Merton but a book about our spiritual journey, for which Merton offers ideas, suggestions and necessary encouragement but in which Merton himself never becomes the object of interest himself.
101 O'Laughlin, *Beloved*, 106.
102 Merton, *New Seeds of Contemplation*, 1-2.
103 Christopher Pramuk, a later Notre Dame doctoral student, considers in his book *Sophia: The Hidden Christ of Thomas Merton* (2009), 'By contemplation "in Christ" we awaken in mystery to

our essential kinship and unity with the whole cosmos – or better, every rock, every creature, every blade of grass within it.'

104 *Pray*, 64.
105 Idem.
106 *Pray*, 66.
107 Ford, *Masters*, 35.
108 Merton, *Conjectures*, 142.
109 Idem.
110 Higgins, *Genius*, 41.
111 Ibid., 43.
112 In Bengtson and Earnshaw, *Wheel*, 57-67 at 58.
113 Idem.
114 *Here*, 135 and 136.
115 Merton, *Raids on the Unspeakable*, 6.
116 Merton, *The New Man*, 147.
117 *Sollicitudo Rei Socialis* 38, in Miller CSB, ed., *The Encyclicals of John Paul II*, 379-420.
118 *Burning*, 24.
119 Merton, *The Hidden Ground of Love: The Letters of Thomas Merton on Religious Experience and Social Concerns*, 564.
120 Pramuk, *Sophia*, 182.
121 Merton, *Conjectures*, 141-42, quoted in Nouwen, 'Compassion: Solidarity, Consolation and Comfort,' *America*, March 13, 1976, 196.
122 Fiona Gardner, *The Only Mind Worth Having: Thomas Merton and the Child Mind*, 203. 'Le point vierge' is a phrase from Louis Massignon, the French Roman Catholic scholar of Islam and the Islamic world.
123 Merton, *Conjectures*, 142.
124 Higgins, *Genius*, 42.
125 Idem.

Chapter 2: Vincent van Gogh, Henri Nouwen's wounded healer

1 Edwards, *God*, x. Edwards was born in the same year as Nouwen (1932) and also ordained in the same year (1957), although he is an ordained Methodist minister. He was, like Nouwen, interested in the psychology of religion and, once again like Nouwen, taught courses in that subject.
2 Higgins, *Genius*, 32.
3 Ford, *Prophet*, 64.
4 Carl Jung, *Memories, Dreams, Reflections*, 156.
5 Quoted in Ford, *Prophet*, 111.
6 Quoted in *Healer*, 83-84.
7 Ford, *Prophet*, 57.
8 *Wounded Healer*, 104.
9 *Healer*, 86. Coincidentally, there is a book on the Bible translator (who suffered from clinical depression throughout his life) titled, *J. B. Phillips: The Wounded Healer*, by his wife, Vera Phillips, and co-author Edwin Robertson, Grand Rapids, MI: Eerdmans, 1985.
10 In addition to *Wounded Healer* going through 19 printings, the phrase 'wounded healer' has entered into the vocabulary of pastoral care. On this, see Todd, 'In Weakness there is Strength', *The Weekend Sun*, 16 April, 1994, D15. See also Renner, 'Modern-day 'Saint' Reflects on Works, Life', *The Hartford Courant*, 14 October, 1993, B11.
11 McFarland, 'The Minister as Narrator,' *The Christian Ministry*, 18: 1, January, 1987, 20.
12 Jonas, *Beauty*, 22-23.
13 Kisner, 'Self-Disclosing Stories in Sermons: A Multidisciplinary Rationale,' PhD thesis, The Southern Baptist Theological Seminary, 1989, 115, quoted in Hernandez, *Integration*, 53.
14 Jonas, *Beauty*, 22-23.
15 See De Bono, *Exploration*, 160.
16 Nouwen 'A response from Henri J. M. Nouwen,' which is inserted in McFarland, 'The Minister as Narrator,' 20.
17 *Solitude*, 55-56.
18 Quoted in *Compassion*, 107.
19 Ibid., 92.
20 Ibid., 94.
21 Ibid., 95.

22   See ibid., 95-102.
23   See ibid., 97-98.
24   Ibid., 99.
25   Ibid., 99, 102.
26   *Solitude*, 39-43.
27   LaNoue, *Legacy*, 128.
28   On the influence of Van Gogh on Nouwen, see also O'Laughlin, *Beloved*, 97-104.
29   Edwards, *Van Gogh and God*, ix and x.
30   Quoted in Bengtson and Earnshaw, *Wheel*, 112.
31   Ibid., 113.
32   Harris, *The Masterworks of Van Gogh*, 26.
33   *Letter* 79, quoted in Edwards, *Shoes*, 19.
34   *Compassion*, 61.
35   *Letter* 133, quoted in Edwards, *Shoes*, 20-21.
36   Erickson, *At Eternity's Gate*, 56.
37   Harris, *Masterworks*, 17.
38   Quoted in Higgins, *Genius*, 38. Italics added.
39   Edwards, *Shoes*, 10.
40   *Bread*, 34.
41   Billy, *Under the Starry Night*, 13.
42   Quoted in Edwards, *Shoes*, 10.
43   Ibid., 6.
44   Edwards, *Van Gogh and God*, x.
45   Twomey and Pomerleau, *Remembering*, 115.
46   *Compassion*, 62.
47   Nouwen, *The Genesee Diary: Report from a Trappist Monastery,* New York: Doubleday, 1976; Garden City, NY: Image Books, 1981, Doubleday, 1989, London: Darton, Longman and Todd, 1995, 2008. See also Luke Penkett, 'The Genesee Diary' (Book Review), *The Heythrop Journal*, 51/3, May, 2010, 536-38. The review also discusses Nouwen, *Peacework: Prayer, Resistance, Community*, Maryknoll, NY: Orbis Books, 2005.
48   Nouwen, *A Cry for Mercy: Prayers from the Genesee*, New York, NY: Doubleday and Dublin: Gill and Macmillan, 1981; Maryknoll, NY: Orbis Books 1994.
49   On Nouwen's sabbaticals at the Genesee, see Beumer, *Seeking*, 42.
50   On Nouwen at Genesee, see also O'Laughlin, *Vision*, 67-77; Twomey and Pomerleau, *Remembering*, 11-19; and Ford, *Prophet*, 127-35.
51   Nouwen, *Reaching Out: The Three Movements of the Spiritual Life*, New York, NY: Doubleday, 1975, London: William Collins, 1976, 1986 edition, *Reaching Out: a special edition of the spiritual classic including Beyond the mirror with a personal appreciation by Gerard W. Hughes*. London: Font, 1998.
52   *Reaching Out*, 7.
53   LaNoue, *Legacy*, 25.
54   On the three relationships, see Durback, *Seeds of Hope*, xxxii-xxxiii, and LaNoue, *Legacy*, 25.
55   Nouwen was invited to write the Foreword for Edward R. Dufresne, *Partnership: Marriage and the Committed Life.*
56   Garvey, 'An Interview with Henri Nouwen,' quoted in Higgins, *Genius*, 57-58.
57   Edwards, *Shoes*, 10.
58   Idem.
59   Edwards, *Van Gogh and God*, x.
60   Nouwen quoted in Ford, *Prophet*, 20.
61   Edwards, *Van Gogh and God*, 68-69.
62   Van Gogh, *Letters*, 1: 495.
63   Van Gogh's sermon, in Van Gogh, *Letters*, 1: 87-88.
64   Quoted in Harris, *Masterworks*, 41.
65   Ibid., 209.
66   Berry, 'Compassion in the Lives of Vincent van Gogh and Henri Nouwen,' 111-21, in Bengtson and Earnshaw, *Wheel*, 113.
67   *Letter* 405, in Van Gogh, *Letters*, 2: 372.
68   *Compassion*, 42.
69   *Letter* 404, in Van Gogh, *Letters*, 2: 371.
70   *Letter* 218, in ibid., 1: 416.
71   Erickson, *Gate*, 69-70. See also, Nouwen, *Return*, 54.

72   *Compassion*, 64.
73   *Letter* 143a, in Van Gogh *Letters*, 1: 230.
74   *Compassion*, 63.
75   Ibid., 64.
76   On Christ as Servant, see Nouwen, *Compassion:* 23-24, and 27-31.
77   Harris, *Masterworks*, 65-66. On Van Gogh's reading of the literature of his time, see Sund, *True to Temperament: Van Gogh and French Naturalist Literature*. On the juxtaposition of the Bible and Zola in this painting, see Edwards, *Shoes*, 149, n. 20.
78   On the Suffering Servant, see, *inter alia, Healer, Way, Name, Life,* and *Voice*.
79   *Compassion*, 13.
80   Ibid., 14.
81   Idem. Italics added.
82   Idem. It is in accepting this 'divine solidarity' that the heart may be opened to the presence of others. LaNoue briefly refers to the importance of hope in LaNoue, *Legacy*, 91 and 129.
83   *Compassion*, 14.
84   Idem.
85   *Compassion*, 18.
86   We see, here, a significant correspondence with the thinking of both Nouwen and Vanier.
87   Nouwen, 'Compassion: Solidarity, Consolation, and Comfort,' *America*, 13 March, 1976, 196.
88   Ibid., 196.
89   Ibid., 198.
90   Ibid., 199.
91   Ibid., 200.
92   *Compassion*, 73.
93   On Van Gogh and compassion, see also Berry, 'Compassion in the Lives of Vincent van Gogh and Henri Nouwen,' in Bengtson and Earnshaw, *Wheel*, 110-121.
94   On Van Gogh and downward mobility, see Thomas Petriano, 'Henri, Rembrandt, and Vincent: Three Kindred Spirits,' in Twomey and Pomerleau, *Remembering*, 110-115.
95   Consider, for instance, the significance of the absence of light within the church in *Starry Night*.
96   Quoted in Harris, *Masterworks*, 66-67.
97   Erickson, *Gate*, 74.
98   *Letter* 441, in Van Gogh *Letters*, 2: 462.
99   Quoted in Edwards, *Van Gogh and God*, 162.
100 Bengtson and Earnshaw, *Wheel*, 119.
101 *Letter* 132, in Van Gogh *Letters*, 1: 191.
102 Bengtson and Earnshaw, *Wheel*, 112.
103 Edwards, *Van Gogh and God*, xi.
104 *House*, 41.
105 *Journey*, 164.
106 *Compassion*, 31.
107 Ibid., 32.
108 *Here and Now*, 104.
109 *Compassion*, 25.
110 Ibid., 23-24.
111 LaNoue briefly refers to the importance of dependence on God in LaNoue, *Legacy*, 128.
112 *Compassion*, 26. Italics added.
113 Ibid. Cf: O'Laughlin, *Jesus*, 8.
114 *Compassion*, 26.
115 Brett Grainger, 'Henri: A Heart's Desire,' *Sojourners* 25, November-December, 1966, 26-30, 29.

Chapter 3: Jean Vanier and the invitation to come and discover the treasure of the poor

1   Quoted in *Road*, 2.
2   Idem.
3   Quoted in LaNoue, *Legacy*, 34-35.
4   *Road*, 1-2.
5   Ibid., 2.
6   Quoted in Ford, *Prophet*, 150-51.
7   *Road*, 2.

8   See Vesey, 'Nouwen's Difficult Journey,' *The Tablet*, 19 May, 1983, 1, and Goulet, 'Father Nouwen on Nicaragua,' *The Church World*, 29 September, 1983, 3, 12-13.

9   See Meehan, 'He Pleads, Knowing the Charge to Come,' *The Philadelphia Inquirer*, 13 August, 1983, A9. On Nouwen as peacemaker, see O'Laughlin, *Vision*, 96-99; and Twomey and Pomerleau, *Remembering* , 45-58.

10   On Nouwen's visit to Trosly-Breuil, see LaNoue, *Legacy*, 34. See Dear, *Peace*, 153.

11   On Nouwen at l'Arche, see Beumer, *Seeking*, 66-72; O'Laughlin, *Vision*, 105-09; and Ford, *Prophet*, 169-76, and 186-201.

12   Vanier, *Together*, 370. One of the finest introductions to Père Thomas is Nouwen's Foreword to Thomas Philippe's *The Contemplative Life*, vii-x. It also throws much light on Père Thomas's compassion experienced by Nouwen during his breakdown.

13   *Road*, 1. See also Beumer, *Seeking*, 55-56.

14   Nouwen, *Love in a Fearful Land: A Guatamalan Story*, Notre Dame Ind.: Ave Maria Press, 1985; rev. ed. Maryknoll, NY: Orbis, 2006.

15   Quoted in Durback, *Seeds*, xviii.

16   Quoted in Ford, *Prophet*, 151.

17   Wakefield, 'Spiritual Impact: Encounters with Henri Nouwen,' *Christian Century* 114, 19-26 March, 1997, 301.

18   Jonas, *Writings*, xlviii.

19   Vanier, *From Brokenness to Community*, 1-2.

20   Quoted in Earnshaw, *Archives*, 12.

21   *Name*, 10-11.

22   In a letter from Joe Egan of L'Arche Daybreak, quoted in Ford, *Prophet*, 94-95.

23   See Uhler, 'From Harvard to l'Arche: Henri Nouwen Shares His Journey,' *Catholic Herald*, 23 July, 1987, 1.

24   Nouwen, *Lifesigns: Intimacy, Fecundity, and Ecstasy in Christian Perspective = In the House of the Lord: The Journey from Fear to Love*, New York: 1986; New York, NY: Doubleday and London: Darton, Longman and Todd, Image Books, 1990, 2003.

25   Nouwen, *Behold the Beauty of the Lord: Praying with Icons*, Notre Dame IN: Ave Maria Press, 1987; revised 2007 (but only presenting the illustrations differently). In addition to his well-known writing on Rembrandt, Nouwen had a great love for the work of Van Gogh and wrote the foreword for Cliff Edwards, *Van Gogh and God*. On Nouwen, Rembrandt and Van Gogh, see Twomey and Pomerleau, *Remembering*, 105-18. During this period Nouwen also wrote the foreword for Vanier, *Man and Woman He Made Them*.

26   *Marc*, 73.

27   Ibid., 36.

28   Ibid., 41-42.

29   Ibid., 43.

30   Uhler, 'From Harvard to L'Arche: Henri Nouwen Shares His Journey,' *Catholic Herald*, 23 July, 1987, 1.

31   9 October, 1985, *Road*, 43.

32   Quoted in Higgins, *Genius*, 92.

33   Vanier, *Together*, 370.

34   13 December, 1985, *Road*, 94-95.

35   Ibid., 95.

36   Nouwen, 'The Trusting Heart & The Primacy of the Mystical Life,' *New Oxford Review*, October, 1986, 6, quoted in Ford, *Masters*, 77.

37   Ibid. 77.

38   It is pertinent to note here that Newman chose 'heart speaks unto heart' as the motto to be on his coat of arms when he became a Cardinal in 1879. At the time, Newman mistakenly thought these words came from Thomas à Kempis's *Imitation of Christ*. They are taken from St Francis de Sales (1567–1622), whom both Newman and Nouwen revered.

39   *Heart*, 13.

40   Ibid., 62.

41   *The Road to Daybreak: A Spiritual Journey*, New York, NY: Doubleday, 1988, London: Darton, Longman and Todd, 1989, 1st Image Books, 1990. On Nouwen at L'Arche Daybreak, see Beumer, *Seeking*, 66-72; O'Laughlin, *Vision*, 114-35; Twomey and Pomerleau, *Remembering* , 119-37; and Ford, *Prophet*, 169-201, and 213-20.

42   On Nouwen living alongside people with and without learning disabilities at L'Arche Daybreak, see Witvoet, 'Profile,' *Calvinist Contact*, 23 October, 1987, 10-11. See also Kravalis, 'At Home with Henri Nouwen – A Visit to Daybreak,' *The Presbyterian Record*, April, 1989, 24; and Odell, 'Father Nouwen

Sees the Light at Daybreak,' *Our Sunday Visitor*, 12 July, 1992, 5. For a more recent commentary on Nouwen at L'Arche Daybreak, see Higgins, *Genius*, 87-101.

43   Quoted in Earnshaw, *Archives*, 14.
44   *Adam: God's Beloved* completed by Sue Mosteller, Maryknoll, NY: Orbis and London: Darton, Longman and Todd, 1997. See also 'Adam's Peace,' *World Vision*, August-September, 1988, 4-7.
45   Elizabeth Buckley in a recorded interview with Ford, *Prophet*, 176
46   Idem.
47   *Name*, 11
48   9 September, 1985, *Road*, 22.
49   Mosteller in a recorded interview with Ford, *Prophet*, 170.
50   Mosteller interviewed by Karen Pascal on the video *Straight to the Heart: The Life of Henri Nouwen*, Markham, Ontario: Windborne Productions, 2001.
51   Told to me by Higgins, January, 2013.
52   Mosteller interviewed by Karen Pascal on *Straight to the Heart: The Life of Henri Nouwen*.
53   Bastedo, 'Henri and Daybreak: A Story of Mutual Transformation,' in Porter, *Befriending*, 28.
54   Ibid., 169.
55   On Nouwen encountering the 'dark night of the soul', see Greene, 'An Interview with Catholic Priest Writer Henri Nouwen,' *SBC Today*, September, 1990, 10.
56   Ford, *Prophet*, 176.
57   Nouwen also, at different times of his life, stayed at Brook Place, the home and ecumenical centre of South Park Community Trust, a British charity, of Bart and Patricia Gavigan.
58   Ford, *Prophet*, 170.
59   Vanier, *Together*, 370.
60   *Journey*, 51. That God is a source of salvation for all 'is a long-sought-after source of hope for a Church that exists for the entire human family' see Spink, *Universal*, 147.
61   *Here*, 109.
62   Higgins, *Genius*, 64.
63   *Compassion*, 19.
64   Ibid., 17-18.
65   Ibid., 19-20.
66   Ibid., vii.
67   1 November, 1995, *Journey*, 46.
68   Ibid., 50-51.
69   Ibid., 51.
70   Idem.
71   10 November, 1995, Ibid., 51.
72   Vanier had been professor of philosophy at St Michael's College, Toronto, when, in 1964, he decided to leave the academic world and invited three men with mental disabilities to move into his home in Trosly-Breuil, near Compiègne, in France. Vanier himself told me that only two of the three men remained with him.
73   Argan, 'Nouwen finds a home,' *Western Catholic Reporter*, 21 March, 1994, 6.
74   Coady, 'Nouwen finds rest at Daybreak,' *Catholic New Times*, 23 November, 1986, 3.
75   Boers, 'From the House of Fear to the House of Love: An Encounter with Henri Nouwen,' Unpublished, n.d., Henri Nouwen Archives, Yale Divinity School Library.
76   Quoted in Durback, *Seeds*, xviii.
77   *House*, 8.
78   For a reference to downwardly mobile assistants in L'Arche, see Ford, *Masters*, 99.
79   LaNoue, *Legacy*, 131.
80   *Marc*, 35-36.
81   *History*, 2.
82   Idem.
83   Higgins, *Genius*, 88.
84   Ibid., 100.
85   Ibid., 56.
86   Ibid., 78.
87   Ibid., 84.
88   Told to me by Higgins, January, 2013.
89   Since my doctoral thesis focuses on Nouwen and ecumenism, I have not dealt at length with the interface between compassion and ecumenism here. *Finding One Another in Christ: Ecumenism in the Life and Writing of Henri J.M. Nouwen* (2013) may be found in the library of Lambeth Palace, London.

90   *Burning*, 75.
91   *Compassion*, 57.
92   Ford, *Prophet*, 68-69.
93   At the time of writing, Joe Egan is Vice National Leader for L'Arche Canada.
94   Told to me by Higgins, January, 2013.
95   Vanier, 'A Gentle Instrument of a Loving God,' in Porter, *Befriending*, 265.
96   Nouwen, 'Adam's Peace,' *World Vision*, August-September, 1988, 6.
97   Marcus, *In Search of the Spiritual. Gabriel Marcel, Psychoanalysis, and the Sacred*, 105.
98   Quoted in Higgins, *Genius*, 97.
99   Kravalis, 'At Home with Henri Nouwen – a Visit to Daybreak,' *The Presbyterian Record*, April, 1989, 23-25, 25.
100 Nouwen, 'Adam's Peace,' *World Vision*, August-September, 1988, 4-7, 7.
101 *Road* (1985-86, published 1988), *Heart* (1985-86, published 1989), *Brieven aan Marc* (1986, published 1987), *The Voice* (1988, published 1996), *Name* (1987-89, published 1989), ET of *Brieven aan Marc* by Hubert Hoskins as *Marc* (1988, published the same year), *Return* (1988, published 1992) *Jesus* (1988, published 1993), *Mirror* (1990, published the same year), *Walk* (1990, published the same year), *Life* (1992, published the same year), *Gift* (1994, published the same year), *Burning* (1994, published the same year), *Here* (1994, published the same year), *Bread* (1995, published 1996), *Path* (1995, published 2001), *Cup* (1995-96, published 1996), *Journey* (1995-96, published 1998) and *Adam* (1996, published 1997).
102 *History*, 2.
103 Ford, *Masters*, 83.
104 O'Laughlin, *Vision*, 150.
105 Idem.
106 Idem.
107 Idem.
108 *Life*, 41-42.
109 Vanier, 'A Gentle Instrument of a Loving God,' in Porter, *Befriending*, 265.
110 Bastedo, 'Henri and Daybreak: A Story of Mutual Transformation,' in Porter, ibid., 35.
111 *Compassion*, 112-13.
112 Ibid., 113-14.
113 *House*, 23.
114 Idem.
115 *House*, 29.
116 Ibid., 20.
117 Vanier, *Together*, 370.
118 *Here*, 23.
119 *Life*, 48.
120 Ibid., 49.
121 Ibid., 49-50.
122 Ibid., 50.
123 Ibid., 59.
124 Told to me by Higgins, January, 2013.
125 *Gift*, 66.
126 *Adam*, 96-97.
127 Quoted in Higgins, *Genius*, 97-98.
128 Quoted in ibid., 97.
129 Bastedo, 'Henri and Daybreak: A Story of Mutual Transformation,' in Bastedo, *Befriending* 27-35, 32.
130 Ibid., 32-33.
131 Ibid., 33.
132 Ibid., 34.
133 Witvoet, 'Profile', *Calvinist Contact*, 23 October, 1987, 10-11, 11.
134 Vanier, *Together*, 370.
135 Ford, *Prophet*, 195.
136 O'Laughlin, *Vision*, 168.
137 Ford, *Prophet*, 187.
138 Bastedo, 'Henri and Daybreak: A Story of Mutual Transformation,' in Bastedo, *Befriending*, 27-35, 335.
139 27 March, 1986, *Road*, 158-60. See also Allchin's chapter, 'The Sacraments in L'Arche,' in Young, *Encounter the Mystery: Reflections on L'Arche and Living with Disability*, 101-18.
140 In a private communication from Mosteller to me.

141 *House*, 75-76.
142 Ibid., 76.
143 Pramuk, *Sophia*, 80.
144 Jonas, *Beauty*, 16.
145 Idem.
146 Idem.
147 Jonas, *Beauty*, 18.
148 Idem.
149 Jonas, *Beauty*, 17.
150 Idem.
151 Idem.
152 *Marc*, 42. On the solidarity amongst the assistants and core members of L'Arche, see *Return*, 137.
153 *House*, 77.
154 Porter, *Befriending*, 262.
155 Ibid., 264.
156 Vanier, 'A Gentle Instrument of a Loving God,' in Porter, *Befriending*, 266.
157 Quoted in Ford, *Prophet*, 217.
158 *Name*, 35-36.
159 Ibid., 36.
160 Ibid., 38.
161 Ibid., 50-51.
162 Ibid., 71-72.
163 *Cup*, 45.
164 O'Laughlin, *Beloved*, 152.

Chapter 4: *The Return of the Prodigal Son*, the human expression of divine compassion

1   Petriano, 'Henri, Rembrandt and Vincent', in Twomey and Pomerleau, *Remembering*, 105.
2   On Nouwen and Cézanne, see *Road*, 96-97.
3   On Nouwen and Chagall, see *Beauty*, 11-12.
4   On Nouwen at l'Arche, see Beumer, *Seeking*, 66-72; O'Laughlin, *Vision*, 105-09; and Ford, *Prophet*, 169-76, and 186-201.
5   Quoted in *Return*, 4.
6   *Return*, 6.
7   Ibid., 92.
8   Ibid., 93.
9   *Here*, 99.
10 *Cry*, 74. The second edition has 'the visible manifestation of God's holiness.'
11 *Beauty*, 54-56.
12 Garvey, 'An Interview with Henri Nouwen,' quoted in Higgins, *Genius*, 57-58.
13 *Return*, 92
14 13 July, *Genesee*, 50.
15 Merton, *The Behavior of Titans*, 76.
16 *Solitude*, 41-42.
17 *Compassion*, 63-64.
18 Ibid., 74.
19 Ibid., 64-65.
20 Ibid., 67.
21 Ibid., 68.
22 For Nouwen on Romero, see his Foreword to Romero's *The Violence of Love*, 5-10.
23 *Return*, 16.
24 *Return*, 5.
25 Nouwen, *The Return of the Prodigal Son: A Meditation on Fathers, Brothers and Sons*, New York, NY: Doubleday, and with new subtitle *A Story of Homecoming*, London: Darton, Longman and Todd, 1992, New York, NY: Continuum, 1995. This was followed some years later by *Home Tonight: Further Reflections on the Parable of the Prodigal Son*, New York, NY: Doubleday, and London: Darton, Longman and Todd, 2009.
26 Earnshaw, *Archives*, 17.
27 *Reaching*, 7.

28 Nouwen's *Genesee*, covering his time there in 1974, was published in 1976, and his *Cry*, a collection of prayers written during a second extended retreat there in 1979, was published in 1981.
29 Merton, *The Literary Essays of Thomas Merton*, 108.
30 *Reaching*, 26.
31 Nouwen's last section is a rich exposition of his understanding of Orthodoxy. The work, with its emphasis on the three movements, was published earlier in a shorter version as 'Hospitality' in *Monastic Studies*, no. 10, Easter, 1974, 1-28.
32 *Return* was published in 1992.
33 *Here* was published in 1994.
34 *Return*, 15-16.
35 Ibid., 16.
36 Idem.
37 Idem.
38 *Return*, 18.
39 Idem.
40 *Return*, 17.
41 Idem.
42 Idem.
43 *Hands*, 114. The 1995 edition has, 'Compassion is possible when it has its roots in prayer. For in prayer you do not depend on your own strength, nor on the good will of another, but only on your trust in God. That is why prayer makes you free to live a compassionate life even when it does not evoke a grateful response or bring immediate rewards,' 93.
44 *Here*, 23.
45 23 September, *Genesee*, 123.
46 In another book of the same year, *Aging*, and in a product of Nouwen's final years, *Gift* (1994), Nouwen writes at length on how to care for others.
47 *Compassion*, 54.
48 Ibid., 55-56.
49 Ibid., 56-57.
50 Ibid., 61.
51 *Return*, 13.
52 Petriano, 'Henri, Rembrandt, and Vincent,' in Twomey and Pomerleau, *Remembering* , 110.
53 Ibid., 50-51. See Mt 18: 20.
54 *Return*, 21.
55 On Rembrandt and resting in God, see Petriano, 'Henri, Rembrandt, and Vincent: Three Kindred Spirits,' in Twomey and Pomerleau, *Remembering*, 106-10.
56 *Return*, 6.
57 Idem.
58 Idem.
59 *Return*, 7.
60 Idem.
61 On the consolation that Nouwen received on reading the life of Rembrandt, see *Return*, 21.
62 On the peace evoked in the viewer, see *Return*, 37.
63 *Here*, 99.
64 *Return*, 87.
65 *Walk*, x.
66 *Return*, 123.
67 *Here*, 103.
68 *Return*, 104.
69 Ibid., 15.
70 Ibid., 16.
71 Ibid., 17.
72 Ibid., 12.
73 Ibid., 18.
74 Ibid., 14.
75 Idem.
76 Nouwen, 'L'Arche and the heart of God,' 151-60, in Dear, *Peace*, 159.
77 *History*, 2.
78 Idem.
79 *Compassion*, 103.
80 Ibid., 104-105.

81 Ibid., 106.
82 Ibid., 107.
83 Ibid., 109-10.
84 Bonhoeffer, *Life Together*, 86, quoted in *Compassion*, 112.
85 *Here*, 110.
86 Idem.
87 Merton, in his *An Introduction to Christian Mysticism*, 60, argues that divinisation is not only the result of the Incarnation but the very purpose of the Incarnation.
88 *Return*, 135.
89 *Compassion*, 35.
90 Barth, *Church Dogmatics*, IV/1, 201, quoted in *Compassion*, 33.
91 *Compassion*, 35.
92 Ibid., 36-37.
93 Ibid., 37.
94 Ibid., 44-45.
95 Ibid., 135.
96 Ibid., 139.
97 Ibid., 141.
98 Schlabach, *Unlearning*, 145.
99 *Gaudium et spes*, 41-44, quoted in Merkle, *Being Faithful*, 105.
100 Told me by Higgins, January, 2013.
101 On Nouwen's death, see O'Laughlin, 'Henri Nouwen in Life and Death,' *America* 163 (10 May, 1997), 18-20.
102 *Journey*, 53.

Closing thoughts

1 A few of the paragraphs from *History* are published in Dear, *Peace*.
2 *History*, 2.
3 Idem.
4 *History*, 1.
5 Idem.
6 Idem.
7 Idem.
8 Idem.
9 *History*, 2.
10 Ibid., 1.
11 Idem.
12 *History*, 2.
13 Idem.
14 O'Laughlin, *Beloved*, 129-30.
15 *History*, 2.
16 *Journey*, 187. Earlier in *Journey* Nouwen makes the comment, 'For me it is hard to celebrate the Eucharist in a formal or ritualistic way', 80. See Nouwen on the formality of the ritual in *Journey* 84-85 and 199.
17 *Mirror*, 53.
18 Ibid., 57.
19 Ibid., 59.
20 Idem.
21 *Mirror*, 73.
22 Okhuijsen's *In Heaven there are no Thunderstorms: Celebrating the Liturgy with Developmentally Disabled People*, 6.

Integrated Chronological Bibliography

1 Any bibliography of Nouwen's publications presents problems to the researcher, as even the briefest of glances at published bibliographies will show. Some of the original titles have been changed over time and certain works have been combined in new editions. Differences of opinion over whether or not such and such a book should be included in a bibliography of primary texts abound. The following integrated Chronological Bibliography is based on the corpus compiled by Gabrielle Earnshaw, Curator of the Henri J.M. Nouwen Archives and Research Collection John M. Kelly Library, University of St Michael's College in the University of Toronto in her *The Henri J. M. Nouwen*

Archives and Research Collection (2011) (hereinafter referred to as Earnshaw, *Archives*), and lists all thirty-nine books that Nouwen had written and intended to be published in book form in English during his lifetime, including those he was working on in 1996 that were incomplete and published in book form posthumously. Details of editors etc. of these are given in the bibliography. The books are in order of composition, not publication, with approximate dates given for their writing.

Compilations of Nouwen's writings fall into different categories and these categories frequently overlap. Examples of these include 'anthologies', 'excerpts', 'meditations', 'readers', 'readings', 'reflections' and 'writings', including booklets in the Henri Nouwen Spirituality Series published by Upper Room Books, Nashville, TN, over the past decade.

A selective list of Nouwen's articles may be found in LaNoue, *Legacy*, 157-61. These, with very few exceptions, were not used in the preparation of this book since Nouwen had a habit of publishing articles, mainly in order to either receive feedback or publicise a new publishing venture, and then writing books that drew on these articles. Thus, much of the detail found in the articles is repeated in his books.

In addition to his primary publications, there are over 18 000 records held at The Henri J.M. Nouwen Archives and Research Collection John M. Kelly Library, University of St Michael's College in the University of Toronto, (http://stmikes.utoronto.ca/kelly/nouwen/default.asp) including un-published addresses, homilies, manuscripts, pamphlets, papers, and speeches representing over 150 000 documents and other items, and what Michael W. Higgins describes as 'literally half a Canadian football field of archival boxes' in Higgins, *Genius*, 17!

2   It is not certain how many sessions Nouwen attended. O'Laughlin, in an interview with Gerry McCarthy for *The Social Edge*, says, 'Henri was able to attend some sessions of the Council, be-cause his uncle was called as an expert on Jewish Christian relations, and he was able to attend as his assistant,' *The Social Edge*, March, 2006, which may be accessed at *www.renewedpriesthood.org/ca/page.cfm?Web_ID=797*

3   It is not clear how many times Nouwen crossed the Atlantic in this way.

4   The dates in the left margin give the approximate years of composition. When there is no publication date at the end of the entry, the year of publication is the same as the year of composition.

5   De Waal, in *A Seven Day Journey with Thomas Merton*, quoting Nouwen, who wrote the Foreword, gives 1966: 'In 1966 while spending a day with Joe Ahearn at the Abbey of the Gethsemani ...', 9. Bochen ed., *Learning to Love: The Journals of Thomas Merton*, vol. 6, 1966-1967, 232, gives 1967, which is copied by Ford, *Prophet*, 131, and *Masters*, 91. Earnshaw and I consider Merton's *Journal* to give the more likely year because the date is from his diary whereas Nouwen appears to be writing about his meeting from memory.

Index